Truth or Dare Living

*Wild Adventures
for Your Sacred, Sexy Soul*

Lisa Carmen

Copyright © 2012 Lisa Carmen
All rights reserved.

Photo credits:
Dee Hill Photography

ISBN: 1481167197
ISBN-13: 978-1481167192

For Madelyn,

May your days be filled
with truth, daring and adventure.

I love you,
Mama

CONTENTS

Introduction

Part One - Waking Up, Again and Again

1. Are You Awake?   1
2. She's Been Everybody Else's Girl   3
3. No Wasted Time   6
4. Orchid Epiphanies and Dusty, Dumb, Old Stories   9
5. Your Naked Reality   12
6. The Old You, the Now You, the New You   15
7. Mining for Gold   18
8. Look Again   20
9. Show Me Your Goo   23
10. Support That Doesn't Support You Isn't Support   27
11. Lower the Drawbridge, C'Mon!   30
12. Truly Sisterly   33
13. I Heart My m coOverwhelm?   35
14. What Kind of Woman?   38

Part Two - Messy and Magical, Flesh and Spirit

15. Is God a Drama Queen? Or am I?   45
16. The Sacred Disconnect   50
17. Fall on Your Face   53
18. A Simple Revelation   55

19.	The Tyranny of Boob Padding	59
20.	What If?	62
21.	Born This Way	64
22.	No. More. Shame.	66
23.	A Letter of Apology	69
24.	Be Not Ashamed, Woman	71
25.	Before You Were Afraid	75
26.	Queen or Slave Girl	78
27.	This is What Love Looks Like	81

Part Three - It's Good to be Queen:
Reigning Sovereign Over the Kingdom of You

28.	The Art of Being Blue	87
29.	Just Your Everyday, Run-of-the-Mill Unspoken Terrors of Living	90
30.	Hitting Bottom	93
31.	Your Resistance Isn't Working	95
32.	Top-Secret Strategy for Funk Removal	97
33.	Good Grief	102
34.	Stillness	110
35.	You Say Self-Centered As If It's a Bad Thing	112
36.	Trust Your Own Importance	114
37.	Let Yourself Off the Hook	116
38.	Do Nothing	119

Part Four - Fully, Wildly, Passionately: *Dare to live, really live*

39.	This is Why I believe in Miracles: Because I AM One.	123

40.	For Angels and Lovers	125
41.	Grow at Your Own Pace	127
42.	What's your wild heart telling you?	129
43.	Wildly In Love With Life	133
44.	This Living Fully is Risky Business	136
45.	I am the Boss of Me	139
46.	What if Pleasure IS the Path?	142
47.	Shut Up and Let Me Be Happy	145
48.	Watch Out Below, Plummeting Moods!	148
49.	You're Sexy and You Know It	151
50.	What if I Told You?	153
51.	I Will Not Abandon Myself	156
52.	Buckle Your Seat Belt. Hold Onto Your Hat. It's Time.	161

❖ Introduction ❖

"Life is a daring adventure or nothing."
- Helen Keller

When I was in seventh grade, awkward, uncertain, and incredibly restless, my unsupervised class Christmas party ended up being a giant circle of Truth or Dare. While our tired and disengaged teacher flipped through the newspaper, oblivious to our activities, thirty pubescent, horny boys and girls circled up and began to play. *Oh my God*, I thought, *this is it, my opportunity to BE KISSED*. I hadn't yet, up til then, in spite of the colorful yarns I spun at recess sitting on the school steps, with a couple of my friends, sharing exotic, made up tales of various 'bases' of sexual experience with imaginary boyfriends they, not surprisingly, would ever meet. So excited I was that Truth or Dare day, I went to the girls' bathroom, feathered my hair, applied a fresh coat of Bonnie Belle lip gloss and returned to the circle, nervous, adrenalin pumping, ready for action.

"She can't play!" Someone nominated my exclusion. "She's too young." I was a tender eleven to their twelves. *I wasn't THAT young, for goodness sake.* "No, you can't play!" Others chimed in. I was devastated. I pretended not to care, I would just watch, fine, whatever. I didn't want to play anyway.

Perhaps this explains the beginnings of my lifelong love for the game of Truth or Dare. I grew out of my awkwardness, but not out of my desire to be titillated, challenged, amused and entertained. As an adult,

I've spiced p many a dull party with a good game of Truth or Dare.

I love the idea of daring others and being dared out of comfort zones, of speaking truthfully, intimately expressing what might have never been revealed otherwise. Boldly stepping out of the mundane and into a wilder, more adventurous version of ourselves.

In fact, that's what my life has become. I look at life as a laboratory of sorts. A playground, an improv stage, that we make up as we go along, where each and every moment we have the opportunity to test our boundaries, to dare ourselves to play bigger, be bolder, live courageously, love wildly. Sure, we can stay folded up inside of ourselves, cozy and "safe" within our comfort zones. Plenty of people do. I can't live that way.

By some magical, awesome twist of fate, I have become the type of person that would rather risk than stay safe. When faced with a conflict or challenge, even the desire to retract and contract, I choose to go deeper, even if terrified, instead of folding up inside myself. It's scarier, riskier, out on a limb. But as the old saying goes, *that's where the fruit is.*

How are you living your life? As a laboratory, where you get to experiment with opportunities, choices, combinations, testing things out courageously, not knowing what you might get, but risking anyway? As a playground, where new scenarios and adventures can be imagined and created, always new and colorful, even if you're playing with 'the same old swings'?

Here's what I believe: Life is meant to be sexy AND sacred. I'm tired of "spiritual" ideology that separates itself from sexuality and sensuality, as if there is a continuum, where spirituality lives on one side and physical pleasures of the flesh on the other. I'm tired of knowing that sweet, flawless children are being taught that they are born sinful and that their bodies' own natural pleasures are evil and damnable.

I'm tired of women (and men, too) so disconnected from their bodies that they don't remember their last orgasm or any other form of deeply ecstatic physical communion. I'm tired of women that are so deeply entrenched in their 'nice girl syndromes' they have been completely severed from their own desires and longings.

I'm tired of heartbreaking stories of shame and secrets that keep us bound and gagged by our own refusal to recognize that pleasure is our birthright, that our bodies are the *physical expression of the spiritual.*

I'm so tired of all these old, decaying and outdated modes of being that keep us small and scared, afraid of our own light and hiding from our own shadows. So tired, that I am fully committed to helping *you* remember what deep inside your body's core, your soul's center, you already know- that you are perfect, you are enough, that bliss and ecstasy are your birthright and that there is nothing wrong with you.

This book will help remind you that you were born to shine and designed to savor.

That the world needs your light- the world needs you healed and whole.

As I continue to evolve and revolve, learn and unlearn, grow and know, as my life and my work merge to become my life's work, I become less afraid and more committed to what I know is true.

That it's all holy: *every messy, sticky, sloppy, complicated, smelly, itchy, awkward, bloody, hairy, raw, blissful, ingrown, overgrown, tender, juicy, painful, soft or calloused bit of it.*

That we are here for it all, our embodied spirits and our divine flesh, our flawless souls and our scarred and battered bodies, for better or worse, til death do us part. What a team. Holy, holy. Hell yeah.

I invite you to join me for an adventurous, daring game of Truth or Dare. I offer these very personal stories of everyday living, seen through the eyes of a spiritual adventuress. I challenge you to hold these stories up as a mirror into your own life, to examine and investigate your life's mysteries. To reveal and speak the truth, expose your soft, gooey center.

In fact, this isn't just a book you read. It's a book you DO.

Join us in the private Facebook group, anytime, to reveal your epiphanies, newfound pleasures, discoveries and confess your stuck places. Unlike most books that you just read, and think "a-ha" all alone, and plan your actions but perhaps never take them, the interactive aspect of this book offers something critical in designing the lives we want: accountability. We can make plans and promises to ourselves all day long, but when we make them to someone else, they might hold us to it. That's why people hire coaches. Included with your purchase of this book is a free accountability system. But it only works if you work it. (To find the Facebook Group, search in Facebook "Truth or Dare Living by Lisa Carmen." Request to join the group, and post away.)

DO the Dares offered to you at the end of each meditation, and report back to headquarters with your findings.

This is a special book, one that can change you, crank up your vibration and bring you face to face with your truth, your desires. It can dare you to dive in to your destiny and live your purpose. Your life can be one wild and exciting game of Truth or Dare, if you are brave enough to play.

Life is a hot, gooey, messy, sacred, holy, beautiful, sexy adventure. It's so much 'easier' to stay closed, safe, folded, sleeping, hidden. But good God, so dull. Yawn... Let's stay awake, alive, surrendered and engaged, shamelessly and joyfully living loudly, boldly, courageously.

One last thing: While there are any references that speak directly to women, if you are a man reading this, you can play, too! Whoever you are, you are welcome to join the game. Unlike my seventh grade Christmas party... all are welcome here.

Let's get started. Join the private Truth or Dare Living Facebook Group and introduce yourself. Tell us why you purchased this book or what you are hoping to experience. See you there!

❖ PART ONE ❖

Waking Up, Again and Again

❖ CHAPTER 1 ❖

Are you awake?

*"Enlightenment must come little by little
-- otherwise it would overwhelm."*
             - Idries Shah

I used to think 'enlightenment' was something that happened to you, you 'reach' it, like a place, and then, voila, you were enlightened. The more I learned and evolved, the more I realized that enlightenment happens little by little, over and over.

In fact, as long as we are human beings, full and complete enlightenment may and probably *should* evade us, hence the human experience. I have reason to believe that true enlightenment comes when we are finished, completely done, experienced and integrated, and free from our human form.

But in the meantime, let's awaken. Let's make these matters of living mean something. Let's allow our experience and our insights to transform us, evolve us. Let's pay attention and take notes.

We wake up. But it's so easy to fall back asleep.

And so we must be diligent, and committed to waking up, again and again. Daily, moment by moment, committed to staying awake.

There are various areas in our lives where we might be awake while simultaneously we are asleep in other areas of our lives.

That's okay. We are human, after all. What fun would this human experience be, if we got it right all the time, and just coasted through all of our classes and assignments with ease and grace, not being challenged? Sounds pretty boring to me. Our invitation from Divinity, our challenge, always, is to stay awake. After the breakthroughs. After the epiphanies. Don't go back to sleep.

*"The breeze at dawn has secrets to tell you. Don't go back to sleep.
You must ask for what you really want. Don't go back to sleep.
People are going back and forth between the
door sill where the two worlds touch.
The door is round and open. Don't go back to sleep."
- Rumi*

* * * * *

❖ TRUTH

Name an area, one are of your life where you seem to 'fall back asleep' again and again, even after breakthroughs and epiphanies. Write your truth in your journal, or on the private Truth or Dare Living Facebook Group.

❖ DARE

Do one thing that you've avoided, one step toward that thing you've avoided, in order to stay awake in that one area. For example, if your health is an area you seem to 'fall back asleep' in, call and schedule that physical you've been avoiding. If keeping your home free of clutter is an area you fall back asleep in, spend twenty minutes working on that 'closet from hell'. It doesn't have to be a huge action. You don't have to change the world today. Maybe some other day, but for now, one small shift can cause ripple effects that really do make the difference.

❖ CHAPTER 2 ❖

She's Been Everybody Else's Girl

*"From the shadow, she crawls. And in the shadow, she finds her way...
She's been everybody else's girl. Maybe one day, she'll be her own."*
- Tori Amos, "Girl"

I've been noticing a trend that's common with many of the women that are attracted to the work I do.

At some point in many of our lives, we begin to wake up to the question **"What do *I* want?"**

Perhaps we hadn't been asking it because we were too busy taking care of others. Surviving. Working. Nurturing the kids, taking care of a husband, managing a household, serving on the P.T.A... all very noble and important duties, indeed. But if the connection with our Inner Selves is lost along the way, which very often, it is, eventually those noble and important duties start to feel heavy, or less fulfilling, or empty. Or even like dying a slow death.

And then, from *under the shadow of divine discontent, we crawl*. We start reaching. Searching. To access the passion, the FIRE within us that we have lost contact with. We know it's in there. We're searching, all right, but sometimes we don't know it's *our selves* that we are searching for. Sometimes, sadly, we even act out in dangerous and destructive ways, just to feel alive. Some find religion. Some file for divorce. Some have affairs. Some drink to numb. Some watch too much reality T.V. or eat to numb the disconnect.

And some -- the lucky ones-- reconnect with themselves. And when that happens, ohhh yes... the world cracks open. The ground begins to shake. The old paradigms don't work anymore. Systems begin to crumble. The 'way it's always been' suddenly is outdated.

When a woman reconnects with her deepest truest self, the world may turn upside down on its axis.

If *you* are waking up... if you are reconnecting to that which you had lost, within yourself... open up and allow.

The timing is perfect. *Nothing is wasted.* You are right on time.

But be warned, dear sister. When you begin to take a stand for YOU in whatever ways that might be, the people in your life may not like it. They may resist. When a husband sees his wife growing wings, he fears she will fly away. So he may resist, so things can stay the same... *'safe and sound.'*

And maybe she will fly away and maybe she won't. But there's nothing safe about never changing.

And when the shifts start happening, we can't go back to sleep.

Things can't stay the same.

Our souls won't allow it.

But trust this: everything will be alright.

A self-connected, actualized woman, being her truest self, reigning supreme over the kingdom of her life is a gift. To her partner, her kids, her employees, her family. To the world.

If you are not madly, wildly in love with your life, only you can fix it. As daunting as that may seem, it happens choice by choice. It can start with what you eat for breakfast. Or what you do with that one free hour in your schedule today. It can start with an honest conversation. Or a renewed commitment to finding more pleasure in your life.

You were meant to reign sovereign in the Kingdom of YOU. Who's on the throne?

What pleases you?

What do you want?

* * * *

❖ TRUTH

Well… What pleases you? What do you want? What's missing? Journal privately or share in the Facebook group. What do you want?

❖ DARE

Do one small thing TODAY that will bring you closer to a desire you've neglected. Micro-movements are key in getting you moving toward those desires. One small thing. Then report to headquarters your experience!

❖ CHAPTER 3 ❖

No wasted time

Too bad you wasted all those years in Dallas, when you could've been living in Austin!" read the reply comment to my friend's Facebook status update. My friend had just been gushing about being wildly in love with her new town.

I didn't feel it was my place to respond. So, instead, I turn to you.

Too bad you wasted all those years ___ when you could've been ___ .

Many of us have said or thought this exact thing, though we may fill in the blanks differently. Maybe yours is something like this...

Too bad I wasted all those years being married to husband A when I could've been married to husband B.

Too bad I wasted all those years working for the man when I could've been an entrepreneur.

Too bad I wasted all those years drinking when I could've been sober.

Too bad I wasted all those years settling for less than, when I could have had more.

Too bad I wasted all those years miserable, when I could have been medicated.

Got any of your own to add?

When I read, hear or start to think thoughts like this, my soul stirs and I feel a soul-resistance. It's as if She Who Knows, inside of me, refuses to allow that type of thought to entertain my brain. It just does not compute.

I don't believe in wasted anything, really.

Because it's all gotten me right here >.<.

And right here is exactly where I am meant to be. Right here is that much closer to where I'm going. I love right here, I love where I'm going and I even love where I've been.

Sure, there are many choices, changes, events that I could look back on and regret, but every single one of those changes, choices and events has played a part of bringing me exactly to where I am- and there is no mistake there. No failure. Nothing to regret.

If I am living an aware and engaged life, I can turn any regret into wisdom. I can use my new wisdom to guide future choices or help others. I can view my past experiences as part of my healing journey.

* * * *

❖ TRUTH

What would your life feel like if you let go of your regrets?

If you instead, thanked your "poor" choices and your perceived missteps for moving you forward, to where you are now?

How would your energy shift?

How would your body feel?

It's my belief that regret often manifests itself as chronic pain, disease, addiction.

Regret is a form of bondage.

It is crippling and demeaning. It keeps us stuck, and playing small. At worst, it can manifest as a deep self-hatred, rooted and twisted and stinking and infecting everything to come.

What would happen if you simply let go of any and all regrets you've been carrying around with you?

Where you are now is exactly right.

"*Too bad you wasted all those years ___ when you could've been ___ "*has no place in what's **exactly right.**

❖ DARE

What is one thing you've been regretful about that you are ready to release? Write it down on a piece of paper and burn it, bury it, tear it up... get rid of it. While you do so, imagine that regret leaving your consciousness once and for all. Report back to headquarters with your triumphant tale!

❖ CHAPTER 4 ❖

Orchid Epiphanies and Dusty, Dumb, Old Stories

I was entering the grocery store one day when I noticed a huge display of orchid plants, blooming and gorgeous in their delicate splendor. And they were on sale, for cheap. "Ohmygod!" I thought. "I want one." But then quickly I reminded myself that *I am not the kind of person that can maintain an orchid.*

The cool thing about evolving is that while I still think stupid thoughts like that one, I am getting quicker at catching myself for their stupidity. My Higher Self, a.k.a Magnificent Me, quickly rebutted "Kind of person? You had an orchid plant ONCE, ten years ago. It died. Does that make you ANY 'kind of person'? Really, Lisa?" And suddenly I realized just how silly it was that I had made up a story about 'the kind of person' I was, based on ONE FRIGGIN' EXPERIENCE. Ten years ago.

Who knows, I very well may be terrible with orchids. But wouldn't I need to at least try again, just to see?

This inclination I have to make up stories and accept them as truth is not solely limited to orchids. I do it with other things, too. And I bet you do, too. Go on, think of a story you tell yourself, either about yourself… like…

I am not the type of person who ____.

Or maybe a story you tell yourself about the world.

The world is _____ and _____.

Or about men. Or people. Or relationships. Or love. Or work. Or money.

Do you, like me, have any silly stories you tell yourself based on ONE LITTLE EXPERIENCE?

I decided, right then and there, to ditch the orchid story. Maybe I am a serial orchid killer. Maybe I'm not. But one ugly experience with an orchid makes me neither. It just makes me the kind of person who had an orchid once that died. Period.

* * * *

❖ TRUTH

Think about the beliefs you hold, about who you are, or the way life is, or the way people are. An easy way to find them is that they often have the word "always" or "never" in them. Entertain the idea that a belief is simply a story you made up, possibly based in fact, possibly not. Are you ready to entertain a new story?

❖ DARE

I invite you to ditch a story. Invent a new one, based on potential and possibilities, instead of absolutes and "never" and "always". Or even just simply be open to being proven wrong by a new story, a different story, one that is expansive and healing, wide open and glorious.

Come on, I dare ya.

Pick just one of those stories, expose it for what it is (just a story you made up, for god's sake.) and allow your Magnificent You argue for a new story. Or expose the story for its limited research and documentation and flimsy evidence.

And no, I didn't buy the orchid. But I did ditch the story. And maybe next time, if they're still on sale, I'll buy one.

❖ CHAPTER 5 ❖

Your Naked Reality

Who am I?
What are my values?
What are my needs?
Am I true to myself?
Do I betray myself?
What are my feelings?
Am I capable of love?
Am I true to my love?

Femininity is taking responsibility
for who I am,
not only what I do
not how I seem to be,
not what I accomplish.

When all the doing is done,
I have to face myself
in my naked reality.

- Marion Woodman

There comes certain times in our lives when we are faced with our own naked realities. Where life challenges us to examine ourselves, get completely honest and willing to see things we'd frankly rather not see or admit about ourselves. The way we do things. The way we do love, friendship, life. The way we treat our bodies.

Lately life has been challenging me, in its loving, direct, firm and provocative way, to look closely in my inner mirror. And I don't always like what I see. I don't like the way I've been so busy that my relationships and health have been put on back-burners. Not to simmer, but to crust and harden, for lack of stirring.

The poem above by Marion Woodman showed up one morning, at the perfect time, as miracles often do, as love letters from God are prone, as confirmations of right paths are revealed in perfect timing, to encourage me to continue lovingly and honestly examining myself.

I immediately did three things- three actions *to support the life I want*, not the life I've been living. Action is empowering, and after a couple of crappy days beating myself up for poor choices, I stood up, dusted myself off, and acted in accordance with who I want to be.

1. I called my favorite wellness center, and scheduled a health and nutrition consultation and some Bowen work to begin, really begin, my wellness path.

2. I apologized to an important friend I had hurt.

3. I walked hard and fast for 30 intense and beautiful minutes in my gorgeous neighborhood, and talked to God.

And with courage and honesty, I continue to explore and question my actions, motivations, feelings and thoughts, to pinpoint the areas that need attention, and to act on them.

Lovingly, firmly, "when all the doing is done", I face my naked reality, and remind myself...

Everything. Is always. Okay.

* * * *

❖ TRUTH

How have you been letting yourself down lately? What needs are you ignoring? What choices are you making that do not support the direction you want to be heading in? Share with the Facebook group or in your journal. Write it out. Type it out. Confess.

❖ DARE

Do three, yes three, things TODAY that will support your future desires. That reflect the YOU you want to be, rather than the you you have been. Step up. Take action. DO something loving or your self. And report back to headquarters with your success story.

❖ CHAPTER 6 ❖

The Old You, the Now You, the New You

So many people I work and play with come with a common need: *to reconnect with part of themselves that they have lost.*

I know this feeling. I'm quite familiar with it, in fact. But I also know sometimes that being who we 'used to be' isn't a fair or realistic option.

When I watch one of my favorite shows, A & E's, Intervention, and the family's all joined together to tearfully read their pleas for rehab to their addicted loved one, something they often say jostles me. Many times, they'll say something along the lines of… "I just want the *old you* back…"

But is it the "old" version of them that really needs returning?

I'm not saying I can't or don't relate to the despair of loving someone with an addiction, I get it, on a very intimate level, in fact.

I'm also not saying that I can't understand the human inclination we sometimes have to wish we could 'rewind life' and go back to a simpler time, a more innocent time. I get that, too.

But I also think this: The 'old' version of the addict is *the one that became addicted.* The one that was suffering, and numbing out in various ways, hiding secret pain, secret shame, and heading in the direction of the very addiction that brought them to the NOW. The exact and perfect now, the only place where NEW can begin.

Why not start right there?

So that's what I'm reminded of when people I work and play with talk about wanting to be who they used to be…

"I used to be so free. I used to be so thin. I used to be so confident. I used to be so sexy. I used to be so strong. I used to be so happy…" I get that, too.

But what I also know is this: There is an even *better version* of you than the past version of you. After all, the past version of you became 'outdated' for a reason.

The NEW version of you will be a beautiful and organic combination of who you are NOW, and who you have been.

Take ALL of it… the good, the bad, the strength, the pain, the mistakes, the glory, the extra weight, the laugh lines, the attitude, the insecurities, the lessons, the mysteries, the tenderness and grace that you have earned along the way.

All of it is necessary for the perfect recipe, the magic formula, the miraculous terrain, the Divine Totality of the You that you are becoming.

Instead of striving for who you *used to be*, (she's gone, after all…) lean into the completely NEW, more exalted, more sovereign, more complete, more integrated, more healed and more experienced version of yourself.

And in your *new glory*, you can be thankful for who you used to be, who you are now, and who you are becoming.

Always, you are becoming.

* * * *

❖ TRUTH

How have you been holding onto the past? What are the parts of you that you miss?

❖ DARE

How can you evolve and move forward instead of looking to the past? How can you accept the now a little more, even if it's not 'perfect'? I dare you to take one step in loving the now a little more. I dare you to create a list of what is perfect and good about right now.

Letting go of what was, and embracing what is will get you closer to what you want to be. Do it. I dare you.

❖ CHAPTER 7 ❖

Mining for Gold

"I have always believed, and I still believe, that whatever good or bad fortune may come our way we can always give it meaning and transform it into something of value."
-Hermann Hesse

Sometimes, when I, or someone I love, is going through a crisis, I hear a well-meaning person say "everything happens for a reason." And sometimes, let me tell you, that isn't very comforting. Just the opposite. I think we can really twist ourselves up trying to figure out the 'whys' of our crisis, our devastation, our pain, or random acts of violence, catastrophe, or the unthinkable... whatever that may be. Trying to figure out the 'reason' is almost like trying to take the blame. It can become a fantastic form of masochism.

Frankly, I don't want to believe in a god that hands us lessons in the form of loss, devastation or suffering. But I do think that we are alchemists, and have the power to turn lead into gold, in even the darkest of situations.

Instead, I find it so much more beneficial to look not at "why this happened" but *"what meaning will I create from it? How can I transform it into value? How will I make this matter?"* (And this process should come after we have given ourselves enough time to feel, grieve, cry, be angry... whatever feelings we need to feel...)

* * *

❖ TRUTH

When and/or how have you taken a crisis or even a tragedy, and instead of spending your truly precious energy trying to figure out WHY it happened, instead made it matter? How did you transform it into information or expansion?

In your journal or in the Living Truth or Dare Facebook Group, speak your Truth.

❖ DARE

I dare you to take one particular issue or experience in your life that is causing or has caused you pain, a situation that even now, as you think about it, the feelings of pain, of despair or sadness bubble and rise to the surface. At the top of your page, briefly write about the issue or situation. Then, make a list of at least ten gifts or blessings that were birthed out of that situation, or that would not have happened had you not had that issue or experience in your life. Our perspective shifts the energy of our wound and can be an amazing catalyst for healing.

❖ CHAPTER 8 ❖

Look Again

I have hated carnations ever since I was old enough to realize they are the 'poor man's rose.'

Sure, I liked them in high school, when Valentine's week brought carnation deliveries to homeroom, with notes attached from friends, secret admirers and whatnot, raising money for the marching band or whatever. Not that I ever got them, but I sure lusted hard after them.

But then I grew up, and since that time, I have considered them cheap, simple, trite. Once, way back when, for some holiday like Valentine's or my birthday or something, my then-husband had a bouquet delivered to my office. I got the call from the receptionist... that call we all love to get... "You have a delivery at the front desk..." I eagerly raced to the front, trying to keep my gait a brisk walk, as to not to seem too eager...

I saw it there... a big mixed bouquet of flowers. Most of them carnations. My heart sank. Carnations? A bouquet of carnations? Really? I put them on my desk, and endured an afternoon of lackadaisical comments from co-workers like "Oh... you got flowers. Umm, nice..."

I know, I know. It's the thought that counts, beggars can't be choosers, yada yada.

I just didn't like them. Not for what they looked like, as much as what

I thought they represented. *"I care, but not enough..."* Another story I made up, of course. Applying more meaning behind an event that is necessary or even helpful. (One of my many talents.)

Yesterday, I went to the chiropractor and when I was checking out, the assistant reached behind the desk and pulled out three carnations and gave them to me as a Mother's Day gift. I brought them home, clipped the long stems and put them in a tiny vase on my desk. And now, they are blooming and vibrant and looking at me with love... "See, aren't we beautiful?"

And as I gaze upon them, I realize now how intricately designed they are. Their petals are smooth and velvety, not much different-feeling than the petals of a rose. They are strong and hearty and brightly colored and oh, I may have pegged them all wrong, for all these years. Yes, carnations, you are beautiful.

I'm reminded of the root meaning of the word 'respect'. RE (again.) SPECT (to look.) After a while, our stories and stereotypes and limiting beliefs become stifling. Boring. Stale and crusty. And then, we have the choice to RESPECT whatever it is we'd been holding ourselves back from. It could be love. A career dream. Deeper intimacy with an old relationship. A carnation. When we look again, we might be lucky enough to see differently. With new respect and new appreciation. Isn't that the coolest?

I'm not saying I want a bouquet delivered or anything... I still prefer roses. (Tiger lilies, tulips, daisies, orchids, even sunflowers will suffice.)

But I look at it this way: Yesterday my desk had no flowers on it. Today it does. And those three carnations are just lovely. That counts for something.

* * * *

❖ **TRUTH**

What are you holding back from, viewing with old eyes and old beliefs? How might you show respect?

❖ **DARE**

How might you look again? I dare you to entertain a new perspective.

❖ CHAPTER 9 ❖

Show Me Your Goo

Vulnerability is sexy.

Maybe not 'centerfold-sexy' or sexy by society's 'standards' (*or lack thereof*) but I think there are few things more beautiful, more attractive and provocative and interesting than someone willing to reveal their softest aspects, and unfold in my presence, someone willing to let the tears fall, melt down, break down, deconstruct, and reveal their inner truth, in the interest of truth.

We spend a lot of energy trying to look/feel/be '*strong*'… and I think we are sadly misguided as to what we categorize as 'weak' or 'strong'… for example… someone avoids going to therapy for years because they consider themselves to be strong. If you've ever been in therapy, you **KNOW** it ain't for wimps. It takes **A LOT** of courage to willingly tread forward in the dismantling and reconstructing of all one's stories and painful realizations, and to boldly choose to heal, when staying wounded can feel so much more safer.

I see women often fanning their faces when the tears threaten to fall, as if the right little puffs of air aimed at their eyes might push the tears back in their head, when all the tears really want is to simply fall in a safe and loving space. Let them fall. There is nothing weak about expressing emotion.

If you're hanging out with me, your tears are always welcome.

In fact, when someone cries around me, I feel privileged and honored to bear witness to their vulnerability. Gifted and blessed. Where and when and how we learned that it was dangerous to be seen crying, I don't know. I hate that. Of course, the wheres and whens of how we show emotion, and with whom, are to be kept in consideration... who among us hasn't been "*The Crying Girl*" at the office, later to regret it?

One day, when my teenaged daughter was hurting in the middle of a heart break, I could tell she wanted to cry, she was holding back tears and her face muscles showed it. Her face was red, contorted, eyes swelling with tears. "*Let it out.*" I suggested. "*It's easier to just cry.*" And once she did, she agreed it **WAS** easier. The tears fell freely, the sadness moved through her, she eventually felt better. Of course, as her mama, I'd rather that she never, ever got hurt... *but life is painful sometimes.* And in that moment, in the hurt, she allowed herself to cry. It was beautiful.

Let your emotions move through you. "***Tears are like a spiritual workout.***" My sweet friend told me recently. "***Think of them as sweat for the soul.***"

I remember when I first knew I was falling in love with my boyfriend. He was showing me his family photos and started to get choked up when talking about his Nana. Any man that gets teary-eyed remembering his grandmother has an advanced emotional intelligence in my book, and while few of us want a '*blubbering crybaby*' for a man, there's something quite appealing about a man who is in touch with his emotions, and is unafraid to show them.

In my coaching group recently, several of the women, including myself, at one point or another in that evening's session, let the tears fall. It felt safe and right, and shit, we were dealing with some **BIG** stuff... it would have been weird **NOT** to cry. We felt raw and naked, exposed, real. You could feel the intimacy in the air. It was palpable. And it was beautiful.

Whenever I am lucky enough to be able to hold space for someone in their raw vulnerability I consider myself greatly blessed and I know that that person has just accessed truth, because when truth gets tapped, like a reflex, *the tears come.* Let them come. Let them flow.

When you have found your people, *your tribe,* you will know it because you'll cry and feel safe in your vulnerability.

It takes a lot of energy to hold emotions in, to fight tears. And imagine what we could do with all the energy we've used to holding back our vulnerability, swallowing our emotions, fanning those tears back up into our heads, keeping our feelings hidden.

Let's use that energy, instead, to create safe space for one another, so we can reveal our mushy, messy, gooey parts, in all their sexy realness.

There's nothing weak about showing your emotion. **It takes great courage to be vulnerable.**

Your tears are safe with me. Go ahead, cry. You're beautiful when you're vulnerable.

> *"Real fearlessness is the product of tenderness. It comes from letting the world tickle your heart, your raw and beautiful heart. You are willing to open up, without resistance or shyness, and face the world. You are willing to share your heart with others."* - Chogyam Trungpa

* * * *

❖ TRUTH

When's the last time you had a good cry? Do you think it's time? What have you avoided crying about, or grieving, or feeling? Journal your truth or be even more courageous and post to the private Facebook Group.

❖ DARE

I dare you to cry. Go on, let yourself cry, let the tears flow, conjure up all those sad things you avoid thinking about. Nothing bad will happen to you if you let yourself feel. You won't get stuck there. I promise. Your feelings just want to move through you. Need help to get the tears flowing? Watch Titanic, the Notebook or your favorite tearjerker movie to get the ball rolling.

❖ CHAPTER 10 ❖

Support That Doesn't Support You Isn't Support.

Have you ever been in a situation where you start getting tons of advice from the world, information, offers, stories? For example, if you've been ill, or struggled with mysterious symptoms, or a diagnosis. Or if you've been pregnant or job-hunting, or buying or selling a house, or starting a business or quitting a job.

I've been encountering an interesting phenomenon in recent months, as I've been experiencing a serious chronic pain situation. So many people, in their desire to be helpful, seem to want to tell me what's best, what I need to do, or not do. And while some of it is requested and sometimes even helpful, some of it is intrusive, uninvited and confusing.

Being on this end of the situation, I've become much more sensitive to the way I respond to other people's situations or crisis with a gentle approach. I ask for permission before doling out advice, I make sure to own my own experience as my own, and not attempt to know or speak of what will happen to them "you're gonna this or that, or you'll want to that or this…" And yeah, I still forget sometimes.

I think in any important life situation or crisis, we have to become experts at discernment, we have to become sagacious and sift each well-meaning piece of advice through our own inner sieve, allowing what feels like Truth for us, what resonates or generates a feeling of validity in our core, to stay, and releasing everything else as chaff and letting it fall away.

And in certain situations, we must find our voice, and access our power, so that we can say things like "You know, I appreciate your intention, but today I am at full capacity for receiving advice, and would rather we discuss other things. Cool?"

I listened to an awesome call with teachers and authors Jennifer Louden and Hiro Boga about this very topic- receiving (and sifting through) support, and took away this awesome truth:

Support that doesn't support you isn't support.

It's information. And while information is… well, informative, we are still and always the authorities on what's best for us.

And while our well-meaning friends and family may continue to share solicited and unsolicited advice, solutions, therapies, treatments, ideas, shoulds and shouldn'ts… we must eventually change stations, and turn the dial until we pick up reception for our own Inner Truth Radio Network. Most of the time my Truth speaks in whispers, so I can't possibly hear her, until I turn down the chatter and pull myself away from the drama and Other People's Stories, and place my attention within.

Some call it Intuition, some call it inner voice, inner wisdom, some call it God. Whatever you call it, it's in there, and it knows, always, what is best for you.

In my own life recently, I've made a couple decisions that came directly from this deep seat of wisdom and love within me. It hasn't been easy, in fact it's often been frightening to not just hear, but actually listen, to act and move in accordance to my Truth.

I find my Truth located in my heart area, and often in my gut area. Sometimes it's a 'voice' that I actually hear inside me, and sometimes it's a feeling. Whether I feel it, or hear it, this voice never fails. And if it seems like it's failed, I just don't know the big picture yet. But I trust it. Most of the time.

* * * *

❖ TRUTH

What area of your life do you seem to get the most unsolicited advice in? How do you sift thru well-meaning advice to locate your truth? Where does your Truth live? And can you drop out from the chatter and tune in well enough to hear it?

❖ DARE

I dare you to tell one well-meaning friend, relative or acquaintance in a polite but firm manner that their uninvited rescue, advice or counseling services are no longer needed. You may say something like "Ms. Buttinsky, I know you mean well when you offer me countless cures, natural remedies and tonic recipes for my persistent rash. I've tried lots of things for this, and what I'm learning is that I have an inner physician that I need to learn to trust. I'm tuning in for my own truth at this point in my life. SO back off, lady. Enough!" Just kidding, sorta, but you catch my drift. Report back to headquarters with your experience!

❖ CHAPTER 11 ❖

Lower the Drawbridge, C'Mon!

"The refusal to ask for help is a kind of sickness in itself. The refusal to ask for help is not rugged individualism but ragged individualism and it is a function of fear.

Not that there's nothing to fear. Asking for help is a formidable art and requires that we lower the drawbridge."

- Gregg Levoy, "Callings"

My name is Lisa and I'm a recovering Tough Girl.

Yes, it's true.

My stubborn refusal to request or receive support has been played out in varying degrees of the pathetic, comedic or ridiculous.

Some of my "Tough Girl" gestures have included (but are not limited to)

- Ignoring the guide words in the top corners of pages in the dictionary, because *I could find the words myself, thank you very much.*
- Lying thirsty in a bed because I didn't want to seem 'needy' by asking for water. After surgery.
- Refusing to read directions on Rice a Roni, and ruining dinner, because "Directions? I don't need no stinkin' directions!"

- And of course, who can forget the agonizing dark days when I have stared at the phone, deep in my despair, crying, feeling broken, longing to reach out to a friend, but immobilized. By what? ... Fear of rejection? Fear of appearing "weak"? Fear of being needy? Fear of vulnerability? Yep.

It's taken a lot of inner work, some great therapy, lots of journaling, some incredible epiphanies, and some brave experimenting but yes, I am learning how to ask for support. I am learning how to risk feeling vulnerable. I am learning how to dance with danger by requesting help and receiving it, too. Ooooh! Crazy, huh?

All that tough girl stuff got boring... so now I choose to experiment in the Love Lab of risk, vulnerability and intimacy. So far, so good.

I am learning that the payoff is *worth the risk*: deeper intimacy, miracles and fierce support from a loving Universe and its humans that are *ready and willing to show up for me* (when I lower the drawbridge and *invite them* to show up for me. Wow, imagine!)

Yes, I'm still a Tough Girl when I need to be. And sometimes, when I don't. But those guide words in the dictionary? They sure come in handy.

* * * *

❖ TRUTH

How easy or difficult is it for you to ask for help? When have you needed support but have held back in requesting it? What held you back? Share with the Facebook Group.

❖ DARE

Ask someone for help. Turn to a friend, a relative, someone you're drawn to but haven't crossed that line with yet, and ask for help, advice, company, support. Put yourself out there. Take that risk. It's exciting and dangerous, and you will likely be supported in your request. Unless it's completely outlandish or ridiculous. Report back to headquarters with your tale of dangerous living!

❖ CHAPTER 12 ❖

Truly Sisterly

"It seems to me that if women are going to change the world, they first have to change themselves and rise above the competitiveness we have been taught and learn to be truly sisterly to each other...
It is an article of faith in my feminism that women have to support each other. Because it seems to me that what we're engaged in is a great experiment which is rejecting our society's false definitions of women. We're learning how to create new definitions of ourselves, which includes being sisterly and supportive of each other. We're figuring out a way to forge new paths for ourselves..."
– Erica Jong

I've never considered myself much of a competitive person. Having been last one picked for the teams through middle school might have something to do with that… Things like winners… losers… high scores… I'd much rather work in community on a shared goal than compete against each other for the same prize. I remember going to my first Open Mic in Dallas and finding that poets were being rated by judges with a number system… Scoring poetry? I couldn't wrap my head or heart around it. Which is why perhaps I'm always a little stunned by those unexpected experiences of women attacking women, undermining one another or sideswiping them with less than sisterly acts of rivalry.

When it boils down to it, those acts are simply scarcity thinking, in clever disguise: *There is not enough for everyone*, or even more insidious: *I am not enough*.

* * * *

❖ TRUTH

What are your thoughts on this? What does the idea of sisterly support mean to you, and does your world reflect that? Have you ever been hurt by blood thirsty behavior among women? Have you been guilty of it, yourself?

In your journal or in the Living Truth or Dare Facebook Group, speak your Truth.

❖ DARE

I dare you to approach someone that has acted against you, rubbed you the wrong way, stirred up ugliness in you, or downright hurt you, with love and compassion. Attempt to heal that rift, even if she never knew it was there. Send a loving note or schedule coffee. Do your very best at seeing eye to eye. Put yourself in her shoes and see her behavior for what it probably is/was. Fear in disguise. Mend a bridge. Enjoy how nice it feels. Share your success story in the Facebook Group.

❖ CHAPTER 13 ❖

I Heart My Overwhelm?

Ah yes, I know this feeling: This is the part where I start to feel completely and utterly overwhelmed. I've come to know this place, the Land of Overwhelm. I visit so often, I might as well move my stuff here and take residence. I keep saying I want to do things differently, but what am I doing differently, really?

I look at my list of to-do's and the truth looks me in the eye: *There is no humanly possible way you will get this all done today.*

So I do what the experts tell me to do. I prioritize. I even look at my to-do's and figure out what can be postponed, what can be put off til that nebulous 'After-The-Holidays' time when supposedly everything in my life will get so much easier, and suddenly I will have limitless time to do everything I've been putting off. (Yeah, right.) I shuffle. I cancel an appointment here, a lunch date there. I put off going to the bathroom far too long. (My bladder understands I'm busy.) I've given myself permission to turn some "yes"es to "maybe"s and some "maybe"s to "no"s. I reschedule. I apologize.

And then, this morning, in my journal, I am practicing gratitude, making my list, checking it twice, of all the things I am grateful for in this moment. Doing my best to be present, to stay true to my core, to center myself, yada yada. And Overwhelm interrupts rudely, beckoning… *"Hey! Don't forget about me. What are you doing journaling? Don't you have a buttload of things to do?"* and then I try something different.

Adding to my gratitude list, I write in my journal "*I am grateful for overwhelm.*" Overwhelm stops in her tracks and looks at me with a puzzled expression. I breathe into my overwhelm and decide to do it differently today. I don't need to resist it, to challenge it, to struggle, as much as overwhelm *is* one of my favorite struggles. Today, I'll simply dance with it.

For what is overwhelm, really, but proof of life? Granted, a full life, an overflowing life, and yes, I crave a simpler life, and yes I'd love to take a day of rest-but-there-is-too-much-to-do and yes, sometimes I feel like I am being swallowed, but today, I will practice gratitude for my stress- for the stress is proof of life, too. Do dead people feel stress? Do corpses feel overwhelmed? Doubt it.

There she goes again, even now, while I type this.

"*There is so much to do…*" her mantra, Overwhelm, whispering in my ear constantly, growing especially petulant when she thinks I have forgotten (silly notion- how could I forget?) *"There is so much to doooo…"* she whines *"Aren't you overwhelmed???"* Yes, I am…. yes, I know. Yes, there is. But here's the thing:

***There is* always '*so-much-to-do*'.**

Until I'm dead, of course, and then I'll have an infinite supply of vacation days. But knowing me, I'll probably reassign myself immediately into another body, come back right away, finding my way back into the human race. That will be me, I bet, signing up for this thing, this messy, overwhelming, crazy, busy, stressful, beautiful thing called life, all over again.

* * * *

❖ TRUTH

Consider your list of pending to-dos. Which of them excite you and which of them fill you with dread? What is your relationship to overwhelm?

❖ DARE

I dare you to spend the next day or two in complete surrender to overwhelm. No resistance. No complaining. Just doing the best you can, when you can, how you can. Experiment with good enough. Can you become friends with your overwhelm? Lovers? Loverwhelm?

❖ CHAPTER 14 ❖

What Kind of Woman?

It'd been forever since I'd seen my old friend Gina. A few years back she and I had made one of those quick intense connections that burned brightly and fizzled quickly, though I'd always held her in my heart, we didn't communicate anymore. We were both so busy, her with her stuff, me with mine. Then a couple years ago, we ran into each other in the checkout lane at the grocery store.

We embraced, excited to see one another. She laughed when I asked her what's new. "Well... I divorced David last week." she announced. I wasn't surprised; in fact, I had assumed they had split by now, it seemed inevitable, they had been struggling for a very long time.

What surprised me is what she said next. "I moved out. I'm renting a small room at a friend's house and David has the kids. All of them!" Aside from their two pre-teen sons, Gina also had two young adult children from her first marriage. "Can you believe it? The older two moved back in!" she smiled. 'He's quite magnanimous!' I searched for the proper response. All I could manage was a lame 'wow!' through a forced smile.

In my head, my true feelings quickly rose to the surface, and they weren't thoughts I would share out loud: *What kind of woman does that? What kind of mother leaves her children?* And then, the response, the judgment, the verdict popped up almost as quickly: *a selfish one.*

The gavel cam down in the court of law in my head: *Gina is a selfish woman.*

We left the store together, stopping at my car, a dark grey sedan I've been driving for the last 3 years.

'You don't have the sexy red sports car anymore?" she seemed surprised.

'No...' I answered sheepishly. It was almost a source of shame for me, this new ultra-boring sedan. "Meet my new 'responsible car.'" I sarcastically mock the car. "The Tiburon was my old life. You know how sometimes a possession can be a symbol of something? That car definitely symbolized my Selfish Phase. It was so completely and utterly impractical. I couldn't even drive my daughter's friends in it!" I shook my head, reminiscing. "I was so hell-bent on getting that car, too. But it never really worked for my family. But this car! Now this car is a smart, practical car..." I laughed and we hugged and promised to get together, even though I kind of knew we wouldn't. I got in my grey, practical car and headed home.

My words were reverberating in my head. *'My selfish phase...'* and then, in an unexpected glimpse of truth, I had a new answer to my question what kind of woman does that? *A woman like me.* I am that. I realized I was judging her, and judging her severely.

Luckily, I knew enough about shadow work to know that because she had triggered some strong feelings in me, the situation required further investigation. What was I feeling? I was feeling shame, but I wasn't sure why. My drive home gave me the time and quiet to look within, to question what it was that I felt ashamed of. I knew that within this brief encounter with my old friend and within the feelings stirred up as a result, there was opportunity for growth and understanding and a deeper experience of loving myself, warts and all.

It is often the characteristics we resist or judge in others that serve as a flashlight, if we so choose, to turn within and shine on our own shadowy places. My friend Gina had done that for me. *How selfish of her,* I found myself thinking.

When have I been selfish? Since that day in the parking lot, I have divorced my husband. I have made difficult choices. I have been called selfish. I have probably even had people think about me "what kind of woman". I think about these choices I have made to put myself first, choices to do what I needed to do that were neither easy or painless, but that intrinsically were selfish- *acts of self-interest...* I think of Gina.

I am her. She is me. We all do the best we can.

And now, I'm thinking about the choices we face as women each day, the choices we make to shuttle our children around, serving as under-appreciated taxi services, the choices we make when staring into a pantry, wondering what the hell to make for dinner, how to nourish our families, how to create connection, whether or not we need to be home on a particular night or out with friends, sleeping in late or getting up early to pray and meditate, so many choices that perhaps are neither 'good' or 'bad'... just choices.

We try to make the right choices. The choices we make to stay when sometimes we want to run. And sometimes even, the smart choice we make to run, when we know we 'should' stay... Gina made that choice. I've made that choice, since then.

So what kind of woman does that? A woman with a choice.

I make choices every day that may or may not serve my highest interest; I make choices every day without even thinking about them. Yet they are still choices. And if I am really, truly honest with myself, I can admit that there was a small piece of me that day, in the checkout lane, that felt *envious* of Gina, her new life, her glee, her freedom.

What kind of woman does that? I am "that kind of woman".

We are that kind of woman.

Women who choose, sometimes well, sometimes poorly, women who fumble, who fall, who fuck up.

Women who get back up, who are stronger, wiser for the fall, women who know that *even a fall is movement forward,* and that every choice, from the car we drive to the room we rent, from the ways we love, to the ways we leave, shapes us.

I'd like to make a proposal. Let's make a shift in how we think and talk about being self-centered.

In our culture where it's more popular to complain about your thighs than to praise yourself for being a great person, where it's more in fashion to criticize your shortcomings than toot your own horn, we've created a way of thinking about self-centeredness, that frankly, pretty much sucks.

I'd like to change that.

* * * *

❖ TRUTH

Think of someone you have recently judged. Or perhaps someone who annoyed you or rubbed you the wrong way. Consider specifically what it is about that person, that you don't like, or that you judged.
Examples

-He is cheap.
-She is self-absorbed.
-He doesn't keep his promises
-She whines too much.

Now ask yourself, very honestly and openly, how you are that.
Example:

-How or when am I cheap?
-In what ways am I self-absorbed?
- When haven't I kept my promises?
-How or when am I whiny?

Can you truthfully own that part of you that you don't like.. simply by saying "I am that."? Of course you are not ALWAYS that. No one is. Because we are everything, in our divine totality, we get to be all of it. All those things you don't like, and the opposites of them, too.

❖ DARE

Take this work further, and explore as many traits and characteristics in others that you dislike. Then see if you can look within and examine your life to see when and how you are those very traits and characteristics.

WARNING: Shadow work is not for wimps. But you will only grow by facing those shadows, as part of the diverse, complete and human person you are.

"Do I contradict myself? Very well, then I contradict myself,
I am large, I contain multitudes."
– Walt Whitman

❖ PART TWO ❖
Messy and Magical, Flesh and Spirit

❖ CHAPTER 15 ❖

Is God a Drama Queen? Or am I?

The first time I ever got high was speaking in tongues at a Friday night revival when I was thirteen years old.

There was something so magical, mystical, about baptism in the holy spirit. It would fill me up like root beer on ice cream, a foaming, bubbling energy that overflowed, out of my mouth in electric, mad and psychotic-sounding babblings in a language none of us could translate but a few of us lucky, chosen ones were inspired to speak.

My pastors loved my energy and zeal and this thrilled me. I quickly became a youth leader and visions of bible college danced in my head. I loved it when they'd say to me "Girl, you're on fire!" *I wanted fire.* I wanted to ignite.

Anais Nin knew what she was talking about... "I only believe in fire. Life. Fire. Being myself on fire I set others on fire. Never death. Fire and life."

They were a rowdy, rambunctious, passionate bunch, my church family. I watched them and became them. My earliest experiences with the divine were dramatic, ecstatic, flamboyant affairs with lots of yelling and shouting, flailing around, lots of crying, lots and lots of time spent on our knees, hands raised toward heaven.

"Altar Calls" were my favorite part of church service. They'd happen at the end of service, after the celebration-singing and the offering and the sermon and the slow, serious singing and if God was calling your heart, you came forward to the front, to pray, and be prayed for.

I'd get to the altar and fall to the floor crying, crumpling up into the repentant, unworthy heap of sin that I was, calling out to God to forgive me, forgive me and my thirteen year-old evil ways. What did I, a child, know of evil? Our pastor told us we were all born sinners, that we all fell short of the glory of God, and for years and years, I believed this. So many, many times I was to fall short of this glory of God, and so many times, I'd be on my face, so very sorry, heart torn open, sobbing uncontrollably, broken to bits and feeling so worthless and worm-like, begging God, like a repentant lover, to let me back into His Good Grace.

I have come to learn that I never was broken to begin with. I did not fall short of the Glory of God. I AM the Glory of God... God wanting to experience humanity! (And so are you.)

Along with a tangled ball of beliefs, shame, contradictions, guilt and confusion that took me years to unravel and create a new understanding of God, what the church also gave me was a ravenous appetite for ecstasy.

What my early experiences of God gave me, in that dusty, makeshift storefront church, was a huge God-shaped lacuna in the center of my soul that nothing else could fill, as much as I tried.

I could only find God in the dramatic, in the falling apart, in the speaking in tongues, the crumpling at the altar, the loud wailing prayers of repentance.

Emily Dickinson said *"The soul should always stand ajar, ready to welcome the ecstatic experience."*

Ha! What an understatement. I have lived many of my years in *constant, chronic* anticipation, *aching* for the ecstatic experience. I have sought it out in so many faces and guises and substances and fixes of various shapes, sizes and colors.

My favorite feeling is ecstasy. My favorite place is bliss. But you can't live on the mountaintop, you can't maintain that high all the time. Well you could, but why would you want to? So how disappointing then, to come down, to reside among mere mortals, trudging through the drudgery, ecstasy a fleeting, fading vapor.

What I have learned, since then, is that it is possible to experience God in the tiny and the quiet. God may love to party, but Divinity as I understand it also loves to whisper softly, as gentle as a breeze.

"Lift me up" we would sing in church, our hands raised as high as they could reach, waving, waving for God to notice us. Since then, I have spent so many years longing constant elevation.

We were taught that God only wants his people happy and that depression and anger came from the depths of hell, from a conniving Devil that wanted God's people to fall.

If I didn't already have a deeply rooted sense that all "negative" emotions were bad, I sure would have had one by then. I learned quite adeptly how to abandon myself completely anytime anything less than bliss showed up.

I couldn't stand feeling depressed, or even just sad. So I medicated.

I hated my anger. I was certain it was evil. So I hid it.

I was terrified of my own emptiness. So I avoided it, stuffed it, hid from it, numbed it, you name it. Anything I could do to avoid feeling it, I did it.

I can't say that I've come to *enjoy* emptiness, sadness, anger or depression. I'm no masochist.

But I have learned to stay with myself, to gently hold the feelings that come up, to not run, not hide, to stay put and stay there for myself and compassionate toward every feeling. I'm not done. I'm not "fully enlightened", whatever the hell that means! You will never hear me brag about the death of my ego (which always seems like an oxymoron to me. If it was really gone, would you even know to talk about your ego?)

Nah, I'm not there yet. And frankly, when I do get there, I'm pretty sure I'll be done here. When I'm fully "enlightened," I'll be ready to cash in my chips and leave this casino.

What's the point of being divinity walking around in a human body, if you're no longer human and just divine?

I think that's when we go "POOF" and turn into pixie dust and blend with the ethers.

But most of the time, I know, with a resounding surety, that this life, *my life* is magical, mystical and miraculous, and I wouldn't trade it in for any other experience. I may have work to do, but a lovely paradox is that *I'm already whole*. I am still healing. But I am not broken.

I am still healing. But I am not damaged.

A small voice within me sings "Hallelujah!" half-serious, half-mocking, and I know it's all good.

* * * *

❖ TRUTH

What old stories or messages did you receive growing up, about God, faith, sin or worthiness that do not serve you? Would you like to discard them once and for all?

❖ DARE

Renew and refresh your relationship to the Divine by releasing that which no longer serves you. Create two columns in your journal. Write those things down, for example: *I was born a sinner*. And in an opposite column, write what you would *rather* believe, like: *I am divinity incarnate, and God thinks I'm perfect and awesome*. The coolest thing about beliefs: You get to choose them. Even the ones we were fed when we were children that are deeply rooted. You can pluck them like pesty weeds that threaten the bounty of your garden.

You can take this Dare further by writing those old beliefs on small slips of paper, and engaging in a burning bowl ceremony. In a clay or metal bowl or pot, light the slip of paper and let it burn into ash, symbolizing your release. You can also choose to bury the slips in the dirt as another way to release them. They are no longer part of you, they have no more power.

❖ CHAPTER 16 ❖

The Sacred Disconnect

This spiritual path you are traveling is exactly the one you are meant to travel. All of it is part of the journey. All of it is sacred. Yes, *all of it.*

Often we feel we are on the "right" spiritual path until things go "wrong," and we get bamboozled or sidetracked or take a detour to become an addict or develop a compulsion for shopping or shoplifting or get fired or get divorced or get drunk or forget who we are or take up sleeping pills or sleeping around or sleeping all day and then we've blown it- we're "off" the spiritual path.

Way back in my church days, we called that "backsliding." It was all very black and white- you were either right with God or going to Hell. You were either saved or damned. you were either washed in the Blood or a back-slidden sinner. So of course, we were set up to be in constant struggle, anytime our humanity showed up and we found ourselves less than "Godly." And so began the split, the rejection of selves, the self-hatred and self-condemnation.

I don't believe that to be true anymore.

The addictions, the shoplifting, the eating disorders, the failed marriages, the broken hearts, the affairs, the distractions, the detours, the pain we face in our very complicated, very human lives- it's all part of the spiritual path. It's all an essential part of the journey.

Of course, these aren't the highest, brightest manifestations of our lives. I'm not saying go out, get wasted, rob a convenience store and sleep with your sister's husband just to write it off as part of your spiritual journey. That would be way too easy, and way too careless. Plus, our actions catch up with us: karma can be a bitch.

But I don't think there are any "detours" on the spiritual path, and I don't think we can ever leave it. The only danger to the spiritual path is unawareness.

But you know what? Funny thing is, even unawareness is part of the spiritual path! Atheism? Part of the spiritual path. Suicide? Part of the spiritual path. Cursing God? Despair? Yep. Part of the path. All of it.

All of it, meaning everything.

Your spiritual journey is all your own. It's meant to be exciting and adventurous. Think of Dorothy on the way to the land of Oz.

She had to leave home to find home, just like we do.

She thought she needed something outside of herself to get to where she wanted to be. Just like we do.

She ends up going through all kinds of crazy shit to find her "guru" – the wizard. Just like we do.

Only to find out she had what she needed all along, those ruby slippers, coveted by witches everywhere, to get back to where she wanted to be, just like we do.

As you continue on your spiritual path, I implore you to be as gentle and as compassionate toward yourself as you can possibly be. Keep in mind that it's pretty normal and human and again, part of the spiritual journey, to at times be detached from your own inner voice, to not "feel" spiritual, to be completely disconnected from your soul's language.

Even this disconnect is sacred!

We disconnect in order to feel separation. *Without separation, we would not recognize connection.* We must experience darkness in order to define the light. Without winter, how would we define spring?

Without hot, how would we define cold? It's all part of the great and perfect totality.

If you are looking for a spiritual path, look to the ground. You're already on it.

If you're looking for a guru, look in the mirror. You are what you've been looking for.

If you're looking for your sacred text, look within. You already are holy truth.

You're looking for your way back home? Guess what, Dorothy? You're already wearing the ruby slippers.

* * * *

❖ TRUTH

Consider your path, particularly the way you have judged yourself about some of your less-than-savory choices. Write them down.

❖ DARE

I dare you to create a new fable, one where each "false move" or wandering from your path was actually THE path. What might change in the way think of yourself, or your life? I dare you to compassionately forgive yourself for your so-called mistakes.

❖ CHAPTER 17 ❖

Fall on Your Face

"The spiritual journey is one of continually falling on your face, getting up, brushing yourself off, looking sheepishly at God and taking another step."
-Aurobindo

I should be further along by now. I know better. I can't believe I'm in this place again. Yes, we grow, we advance and evolve, but sometimes we don't. Sometimes we play small. Sometimes we disconnect. Sometimes we self-sabotage. Sometimes we dance with danger and court the illicit and play with fire. Sometimes it feels like we're slipping backwards. I think that sometimes we choose 'darker' because the light is so bright, and we just need some time in the shade, where it's less intense, less illuminated. A respite from our own grandness. Growing up in a Pentecostal church, I was either 'right with God' or 'backslidden'... I wasn't allowed to trust my 'slips' as part of the journey, as equally divine. I believe differently now.

I hate falling on my face. But I'm getting really good at getting up, brushing myself off, looking sheepishly at God and taking another step. How about you?

Dusted yourself off lately?

* * * *

❖ TRUTH

What are some of your 'falling on your face' type experiences, the *"I should be further along by now. I know better. I can't believe I'm in this place again…"* moments that strip you to your core, knock you back a couple notches, humble you and bring you eventually into closer connection with the Divine?

In your journal or in the Living Truth or Dare Facebook Group, speak your Truth.

❖ DARE

The next time you 'fall on your face', ie., slip into ways or behaviors that would not be considered your contributing to your higher good… allow yourself to slip, to fail, to trust it as part of the journey. Then get back up, dust yourself off and pick up where you left off.

❖ CHAPTER 18 ❖

A Simple Revelation

Back in my fundamentalist church days, I learned about the Great Opposition- the never-ending battle between flesh and spirit.

The flesh, they taught us, was where SIN came from, and it was bad, very bad- the body, its desires, its longings.

The spirit, on the other hand, was where God lived. And *you could not be both* in the flesh and in the spirit. It was one or another. Which meant that you were, at any given time, either right with god, or wrong with god. Saved or backslidden. Godly or in the flesh.

As much as I've tried to delete the useless file space in my brain taken up by outdated rubbish like this, remnants of this "flesh-shame" remain.

I know this because it seems that I've often created a distance between me and god when I've truly inhabited my body, when I've let my desires and my fleshliness come to the surface, as if I did not know how to let both sides co-exist and intertwine. I'm learning.

Now, I am choosing new beliefs. I choose to find god *in my flesh* and honor the divinity of the body. I believe in a god that thinks all of me is divine. *I* think all of me is divine.

I am learning to be exactly who I am, and know that is exactly who I'm supposed to be, in this moment. There is nothing to change or fix.

No side to choose. There doesn't have to be this relentless dichotomy. How can I be my fullest self and know that "it is good?"

Ego, ego, all this talk about ego, about death of the ego. I don't want to kill my ego!

I don't want to kill any part of me.

I want to live, to be fully alive- me, my spirit AND my ego, one big, happy, fully-embodied and inhabited human being, for as many days as I'm allowed.

I want to own my ego, and not be owned by it. I want to own my flesh but not be driven by it. I want to fully inhabit this life of mine.

I'm so tired of the relentless self-judgment- all the things I should be doing, thinking, feeling, being; 'AW, FUCK IT' is what I say.

I am ready to simply BE who I ALREADY am.

How to balance the inspired desire to grow, change, evolve with the expansive, soul-affirming desire to simply BE.

For example, when meditation comes up in conversation, there is a part of me that immediately "shoulds on myself": *I should be a meditator. It would be good for me. Why don't I meditate like other spiritual people? I should start meditating. It would make me more spiritual, it would make people think I'm more spiritual, I could be enlightened. Enlightenment! Ooooh....*

Stop: No, maybe I shouldn't be a meditator. You know why? Cause I'm not. And maybe what I'm NOT is exactly right, too!

Somewhere along the line, I picked up the man-made concept that 'spiritual people meditate'. But I challenge that concept with the notion that just as Rumi said there are a 'hundred ways to kneel and kiss the ground,' there are a hundred ways to connect to spirit, meditation being just one of them. I connect to spirit when I walk. When I dance. When I write. Can I stop judging myself for not meditating now? Sure, someday I'd love to be all Zen and chilled, mind emptied, floating around in space with my fingers in mudras, but right now my fingers prefer snapping and typing and touching and doing other fingerly things.

So today I surrender any notion of what I "should" be. Maybe someday I will be those things. Maybe not. If not, maybe I'm not supposed to be those things.

Today I relish the divinity of my flesh, my spirit, united.

Today I surrender self-judgment and allow myself to fully expand into my own perfect me-ness. I'm not supposed to be anything else except this, who I am, right now.

Today I want my actions and my words to come from the most real parts of me- and I want to know that the most real parts of me are the very best parts of me. I reject nothing.

Filled with gratitude for the opportunity to simply exist, as me, right now, right here. Right now, right here, right me- it's all right. It's alright! Even the wrong is right! It's all a gift and today I open wide and revel in this simple revelation: I am.

* * * *

❖ TRUTH

What "should" do you hold over yourself, your spirituality, your life, that casts a grey shadow over your life, does not bring you joy or hope, and just makes you feel crappy about yourself? Share in the private Facebook Group, won't you? Or journal about your shitty should.

❖ DARE

You're on a roll… RELEASE IT! How can you let it go? Another burning bowl ritual? Bury it in the dirt? Write a 'dear John" letter to it? Take action to release that should… maybe it's not the right time. Maybe it will never be the right time. Can you let it go? Whatever action you take in releasing it will serve your spirit well. But don't be surprised if those "should-thoughts" come back, even after a ritual. Just sweep them away like dust-bunnies, and have empowering replacement thoughts ready to respond. Do this and you are one step closer to full authenticity: being who you truly are!

"You do not have to be good, You do not have to walk on your knees for miles repenting. You just have to let the soft animal of your body love what it loves."
                    - Mary Oliver

❖ CHAPTER 19 ❖

The Tyranny of Boob Padding

It was a sexy new little navy blue chemise and I was excited to 'premiere' it for my partner. Its stretchy satiny fabric felt good on my skin, it hugged my curves in all the right places and the light padding built into the chest area made my boobs look fuller and higher.

After a few minutes of kissing and fondling, I got up to use the restroom and was startled to notice in the mirror that the pads in the chest area had become bunched and rumpled and dislodged inside of the gown and now were completely uneven and ridiculous looking! I laughed at myself, yet felt a little embarrassed. *Wait!* I thought. *These can come out!* I grabbed a pair of scissors and snipped a tiny hole on the inside layer of fabric and pulled out the two strange looking pads.

Even without the padding, the nightie still provided enough support and hugged my boobs in all the right ways. I looked fine! Not just fine- I looked BETTER.

And then I had an epiphany. These pads were sending me a message. That message that we women get a thousand times a day in a thousand different ways:

YOU ARE NOT ENOUGH.

The message came loud and clear, I'd been hearing it all my life!

But this time, instead of subconsciously obeying it, I recognized it as a lie. This time, it angered me. It pissed me off with its sneaky subtlety, something so quiet and 'unassuming' as breast padding in a chemise- but still, the underlying message had attempted to taunt me with my "not-enough-ness."

Yet, once I took the pads out, I looked and felt better. My partner's eyes widened when, with my more natural, unpadded look, I entered the room. And of course, I could feel his touch better without the padding. I WAS BETTER off just being me, without those stupid built-in boob pads.

I am not saying we burn our bras and stop shaving and stop caring about the way we look in an effort to celebrate our enoughness. If that's where you're led, awesome! For me, that's way too extreme and I have way too much fun being girlie for that.

My invitation to SacredSexy YOU is to simply be aware of when and how those messages sneak into your subconscious.

And some days, when you are feeling brazen enough, my hope is that you say no to the tyranny of boob pads.

I double dog dare you to grab a pair of scissors, cut out the proverbial pads in your life that lie to you and tell you that you are not enough. That your breasts are not big enough. Your legs are not smooth enough. Your face doesn't look young enough. Your "feminine odor" is not fresh enough. (Floral scented crotch? Really?)

Decide, just one brave moment at a time, that you are not going to be tyrannized by that message of not-enoughness.

Declare, even if just for a moment, that you ARE enough. Because really, Goddess, you are.

* * * *

❖ TRUTH

What lie have you been believing about your own 'not-enoughness'… your boobs are too small? Too big? You weigh too much? Not enough? You're not 'this type' or 'that type'? What dumb old crusty message are you ready to let go of?

❖ DARE

Yes, you know by now where we're going with this! Take action and in ritual, release it. Write it down, burn it. You may choose to go beyond symbolism to the actual source of the lie and release it. Like those ridiculous high heeled shoes that hurt so bad you never wear them, but bought them because you thought you'd look sexy walking around in them. Face it: You bought the lie. Now, can you release it, and actually throw them away or donate them to Goodwill? Like the satin teddy you bought to impress someone, but the crotch area gives you the worst wedgy ever, and wearing it feels more like discomfort than pleasure. Get rid of them!

❖ CHAPTER 20 ❖

What If?

What if you replaced shame with compassion?

What if you replaced guilt with patience?

What if you chose to see the alleged "flaws" in your character as the most tender, delicate parts of you, in most need of love?

What if you decided to call a truce with "that one part" of your body (you know the part I'm talking about) you have spent your life loathing?

What if you decided the war was over, between yourself and your Self?

What if that part of you that's too _____ or not enough _____ was exactly right?

What if you really forgave yourself?

What if you fully embraced the perfection of your imperfections?

What if you loved yourself without reservation?

What if you committed to treat yourself with the same loving care you treat your friends?

What if you decided to stop saying rude things to yourself?

What if you were your own very best friend?

What would your life be like?

How would the world change?

* * * *

❖ TRUTH

In the list of "what ifs" above, which three seem the most preposterous to you, in your life right now? The ones you read that almost gives you a stomach ache, or makes you want to roll your eyes in "Yeah, right!" fashion, or hide under a blanket. Write them down in your journal or share in the private Truth or Dare Living Facebook Group. And do your best to answer them. For example:

Q. What if you decided to call a truce with "that one part" of your body (you know the part I'm talking about) you have spent your life loathing?

A. I would enjoy life more. I would accept pool party invitations. I would no longer worry about people seeing that part of me, and would have more authentic connections and more fun. I would make love with the lights on.

❖ DARE

Write those three questions on stickies, and in your journal and in dry erase marker on your bathroom mirror, stick them in your car, at your computer, anywhere where you are going to see them daily. Allow them to take root in your consciousness, and every time you see the question, entertain the possibility. What would change? What would your life be like? How would you show up differently in the world? Experiment with this for a week, and report back to headquarters with your findings!

❖ CHAPTER 21 ❖

Born This Way

We are born sexual. Sexuality is as instinctual as eating and breathing.

From a very early age, we are conditioned, though, to repress it.

We learn about sex from stealing peeks at necking teenagers and playing risky exploration games with neighborhood kids in the shed. We play with sex by testing our boundaries, sampling... we feel aroused and don't understand why. We orgasm without knowing what an orgasm is (*whatever that was, it sure felt good!*)

We get caught. We are shamed. We are not allowed to express, to experiment... we are taught that "*down there*" is bad... is dirty... is just for peeing. **We are terrified of our own parts. And we are secretly fascinated.**

We learn from our sexuality as much as we learn about it. We get hurt, we get used, we get taken, we get STDs, we have pregnancy scares. We use our sexuality as a weapon, as a mask, as a misappropriated tool for feeling better about ourselves (*Do you want me? Do I turn you on? What do you want me to be? Am I sexy? Am I worthy? Am I good enough?*) We learn. We grow.

And someday, *if we're lucky*, we eventually learn that sex is not dirty or sinful.

We learn to please ourselves. We learn to please others. We learn to accept who we are sexually. And not be ashamed. And not be afraid to be sexual. We then learn that sexuality comes in all shapes and sizes, all kinds of things, places, scents, feelings, situations.

Sexuality can be experienced in a slowly smoked cigarette, or a dance or a smile. Eroticism can be found in the texture and sweet flavor of a ripened strawberry. Sexuality can even transcend gender, to its raw, spiritual core; two souls, strongly magnetized towards each other.

And someday, if we're lucky, we embrace the precious gift of our sexuality, proudly, without shame, or regrets. Without anger. We share our sexuality, coming from a place of wholeness. We cherish our sexuality as a divine tool for expression, for pleasure, for connection.

We accept our sexuality with soft open arms, warm breast and open heart. And in the process, *accept ourselves.*

* * * *

❖ TRUTH

In your journal or in the Facebook Group, share an important aspect of your sexual history. I'm not talking about a list of people you've had sex with… but a chronicle of how you developed sexually, including the unhealthy shame messages you got along the way.

❖ DARE

When's the last time you turned yourself on? You don't need a partner to experience the erotic. I dare you to do one thing today that will titillate you. Report back to headquarters, if you dare.

❖ CHAPTER 22 ❖

No. More. Shame.

When I was in the sixth grade, my parents had this great set of books about "growing up"… which of course, thrilling to me, meant these books were about SEX. Included in the set was a "Parent's Guide" with questions and answers about sex, so that you knew what to say when your kids asked "What's oral sex?" "Is masturbation okay?" This was a goldmine of information for me. I was, of course, very curious about the subject as I knew my peers at school would be as well. The book was loaded with all the good stuff- stuff that my parents, ironically enough, were NOT talking to me about.

Word got around that I brought the book to school. The kids mocked me and said I was a pervert. They called me disgusting. They laughed at me and called it a "dirty book". I became a "pervert that brings dirty books to school."

Needless to say, I was ashamed. Something that had been titillating and curious had once again been made shameful and embarrassing. I was so humiliated, I felt like I could die.

I was reminded of this story recently while reading of the series of tragic suicides related to teens and pre-teens being ridiculed for their sexual orientation. While my experiences, in magnitude, barely shadow the experiences of these particular kids, the bottom line is that I know what sexual shame feels like. So do you. It's painful. It's devastating. It's damaging. And it's utterly stupid.

Sex and sexuality has long been a subject of shame and humiliation, for generations. Most of us, at one time or another, have experienced humiliation simply for being the sexual beings we are.

I'm so sick of it.

"Donna," a client I'm currently working with, would like to feel less ashamed about self-pleasure. She'd like to be able to not feel like her sexuality and her spirituality are in opposition. I am committed to her learning, at thirty-five, that sex is nothing to be ashamed of. That we are born sexual. That our sexuality IS divinity, embodied.

I want to start a global campaign to eradicate shame. It's killed too many people. It's caused too much pain.

Yes, I brought a "dirty book to school" when I was ten. I released that shame a long time ago.

And even still, nearly thirty years later, I am learning to embrace my sexual self as vibrant, rich and holy; as in partnership with my spirituality. In fact, it's all one in the same.

One of my favorite masturbation jokes is "If God hadn't wanted us to masturbate, he woulda made our arms shorter."

While I don't believe in God as a "he," I do find truth in this statement. Everything by design, perfect design.

Wave your flag, whatever that flag may be.

Be who you are…

Curious, sexual, vibrant, with blood pulsing through your veins and sexuality your divine birthright. It's not only OKAY to be sexual- it's what you were wired for!

No

More

Shame.

Breathe into that. Say it out loud. And whatever leftover shame you've been holding onto about your sexuality...

let it go.

Give the world the gift of your authenticity. Start now.

* * * *

❖ TRUTH

What aspects of yourself have you been holding back from the world? Is it time to come out from hiding? Share a secret that will bring you one step closer to your authentic, integrated self.

❖ DARE

Take one action that would bring you closer to releasing any guilt or shame you have about your sexual history. It may be a symbolic gesture like writing a letter to a former lover, and never mailing it, or releasing a secret that has drained your energy by burning it in a bowl ritual. Or it can be a full-out real deal action, like requesting coffee with an old lover for real closure, or dressing in a way that more truly reflects who you are, or scheduling an appointment with a sex therapist for you and your partner, simply to create deeper intimacy. With each and every bold action, we become more and more who we truly are.

❖ CHAPTER 23 ❖

A Letter of Apology

This is not a self-criticism. This is not a cleverly crafted flogging whip with which to beat myself up. I'm coming clean.

This is a letter of apology, to you, my body.

It's becoming clearer and clearer to me that I have failed you, in countless ways.

I have despised you at times, when all you wanted to do was love me, carry me, and care for me in a a million of miraculous ways.

I have ignored your desires and needs. Sometimes for hours, (like *'Hey Lisa, I have to pee… can we get up and pee?'* or *'I'm soooo thirsty. No, not for Diet Coke… can we have some water instead this time?'*) Sometimes for years… (*'Can we dance more? Can we play more? Can we move more? Can we NOT do that again, please? That sucked.'*)

I have neglected pain to be the 'tough girl' when you were crying out in discomfort, only to be dismissed, ignored and shut down. The pain had to reach excruciating levels to finally get my attention.

I have put things into you that didn't belong and were not good for us. Perhaps providing us with temporary escape or pleasure, but in the long run, causing damage to you. Disrespecting you.

I have said and thought the most hateful, abusive words to you, because you did not 'meet up' to some standard that society convinced me was what was desirable, all the while missing the perfections and gifts and love you presented to me year after year, as is.

Body, I apologize. And it has literally taken me 40 years to get to this point, this deep repentance and true desire to finally do things differently. I wish it wasn't pain that got me here. But hey, it got me here. And here is where I need to be.

Body, you have my attention. You have my love. I'm sorry for the ways I've failed you. I promise to make it up to you.

You deserve love, you're pretty amazing, and beautiful, too.

Please be patient with me, as I cultivate this new level of self-love and attention and care. I'm ready now, but new habits are challenging to make, undoing a lifetime of habits is also challenging, but I am supported and have all the tools and resources I need to finally make you a priority. And I finally have the determination. I'm not aiming for perfect. Just better.

I love you. Please forgive me.

* * * *

❖ TRUTH

How have you done your body wrong? Have you abandoned your body? Neglected? Abused?

❖ DARE

Write a letter of apology to your body. It won't necessarily be easy, but it will be healing. If you want to take it even deeper, write apology letters to various parts of your body that have particular association: Dear Hips... Dear Belly... Dear Face... And then, when you are done, do one really loving, kind thing for your body. Take a hot bath. A brisk walk. Get a massage. Report back to Headquarters with your experience!

❖ CHAPTER 24 ❖

Be Not Ashamed, Woman

*"Be not ashamed, woman...
You are the gates of the body,
and you are the gates of the soul."*
- Walt Whitman

Walt sure had it right, didn't he? Interestingly, this was written long before our modern day cultural and media-driven onslaught of the female body, the widespread and culturally sanctioned mass shaming of women and their bodies. But it was relevant then, it must have been. And it is more relevant now than ever.

I imagine Whitman sitting under a shady willow, on the banks of a tranquil pond, with a woman lounging near him. Was she adjusting herself, posing her legs so that the ripples under her thighs didn't show?

Maybe she was pulling her blouse so that it didn't get caught in the soft folds of her belly. Or is that just something 21st century women do, compulsively, without thinking, ritualized and critical? *You know what I'm talking about.* We do it quick. Often. Lest our secret gets out and our midsection is noticed.

I'm so tired of body shame. I'm tired of hearing it. Seeing it. I'm tired of feeling it.

I experience it, inside, way more often than I care to admit. It's not something I'm proud of. After all, I work with women to set them free of their own shame. Yet still, my own body shame lingers and crouches secretly in shadows, lunging at me with sharp teeth when I least expect it. I see a certain photograph of myself. *(Ugh. I look pregnant.)* I get a glimpse of myself at a certain angle (*Whoa, nice chins.*). And that shame, that ugly, abusive voice whips its venomous tongue at me and I am shrunken, beaten down and suddenly flat on my face, splashing in the muck of self-loathing.

Those moments ARE getting fewer and further between. Thankfully.

It's taken me 40 years to learn to love myself, accept myself, adore myself. And I'm still learning. I'm not perfect. It very well take me 40 more years to perfect.

The wicked voice of the Self-Loather is sneaky and subversive. Vicious and cruel. There's something liberating about typing this, knowing that you're reading it. What's that saying? *We're only as sick as our secrets.*

If we all told the truth about the things we say to ourselves, would any of it melt away? Would we feel less alone?

Our society is sick. There's a big, big problem here. We are trained to hate our bodies. We like to blame it on "society"... *society this, society that*.... Well guess what?

We are society. You. Me.

We're the ones who buy the products that tell us we are not good enough.

I am the one with the bullshit anti-cellulite lotion in my medicine cabinet, as if I could just rub it away and then... then my perfect life will start, me and my perfect body.

We're the ones who buy the padded bras because we think our own breasts are 'too small' or not exciting enough.

We're the ones who buy the glossy magazines with their impossible expectations and damaging messages, and flip through them thinking we'll find some holy grail, and all we find is more self-loathing.

We're the ones that spend *billions of dollars* supporting an industry that, as Marianne Williamson says *"does not love us back."*

So when does it change? How does it change? It's already started.

In ways big and small, we are taking back our bodies, we are reclaiming our beauty, our royalty, our gorgeousness.

We are shouting "I GET TO DECIDE" what's beautiful.

And in my little corner of the world, through my work with SacredSexyU and The Burlesque Experience, we are declaring our own worth, our right to strip naked, on stage, in front of a cheering audience. In doing so, we take one step toward healing the world.

Is striptease really that magnanimous and noble? *Hell yeah, it is.*

I like fantasizing about some magical, Utopian day where all women, and all men get to live in a society that blesses and reveres the limitless number of shapes and sizes and textures and layers and varieties of beauty.

And every few months, I get a taste of that, in a special show called The Burlesque Experience BUST-OUT. So yeah, I'm changing the world. One striptease at a time.

Let's change the world together.

* * * *

❖ TRUTH

What lies have you believed about what beauty is and what beauty is not? And which lies are you ready to simply ditch, just like that, right now? Share it with the Facebook Group, or journal privately.

❖ DARE

Take ONE EMPOWERED action, one small step, make one small commitment to repair what has been damaged, undo the lies we have been fed. Research charities that support women and girls and make a donation. Adopt a Little Sister through the Big Brothers Big Sisters in your city. Write a letter to an advertiser that is telling lies to women and girls. Stop buying the magazines. Throw away your anti-cellulite cream. It *doesn't work anyway.* It's a lie.

❖ CHAPTER 25 ❖

Before You Were Afraid

Take a deep breath, and soften your belly. Get comfy in your chair, or bed, or wherever you are reading this. Take off your shoes.

Inside of you is a sweet little child who longs for your love and affection. She wants nothing more than to love you and be loved by you, to be accepted, to be held in perfect affection, to be given complete and total permission to be exactly who she is.

Think back to when you were little, look at a photograph or imagine a memory that jumps to the surface when you remember yourself at your most innocent, your most unwounded… the you that was joyous and ebullient and playful and boundless and confident and brave.

Think back to before anyone told you that you were not good enough. That you weren't pretty enough. Think back to the you that you were before anyone made you feel less than perfect.

Think back to the time before you were ever afraid to express your true nature. Afraid to be wild. Afraid to cry loudly when you were upset or laugh loudly when you were amused. Before anyone told you that the way you were expressing yourself was not okay. That you or your feelings were too much, that little girls should be nice, should be quiet, should be polite.

Think back to before anyone ever violated your personal boundaries or space or body. Before anyone made you kiss that creepy uncle because you're a good girl. Before anyone ever poked fun at your changing body. Before the boys stopped playing with you and started picking on you. Before your parents told you to act like a lady. When you could climb a tree and even skin your knees without being shamed or corrected. When it was okay to get dirty without being told you didn't deserve nice things, because you always ruin them.

Think back to what it felt like to be your true authentic self, before anyone convinced you she wasn't enough.

How old is she? How little is she? Or maybe you can't even remember a time like that. If you can't then she was probably just a little thing, a tiny girl, a toddler.

Now imagine that little self, that bitty, perfect version of you running into the room you are in, right now. She is boundless and beautiful. Brave and bold. She runs to you and crawls up on your lap. Now kiss her soft hair and hold her. Let her nestle inside of your bosom. Let her snuggle you. Feel her hot sweet breath and her little arms around your neck. Breathe in her sweet scent.

Now tell her what she needed to hear, around the time the lies started. Around the time the messages began. Tell her she is enough. Tell her she is not too much and there is no such thing. Tell her she is perfect. She is worthy of love. She is all she needs to be. She is good, very, very good.

Love on her like crazy, talk to her sweetly for a minute every day, because she's still in there, she's still in you, and she still needs to hear those things.

* * * *

❖ TRUTH

What feelings or memories were stirred up by this meditation? How can you love on your inner little girl better, in the coming days? The little girl you called out in the above exercise is very young, and very sweet, and very wild and needs your loving affection. How would you like to express that to her? Share with the Facebook Group.

❖ DARE

Do something just for her. Go get an ice cream cone and sit on your porch and eat it. Buy a coloring book and crayons, and spend 15 minutes a day, each day this week, coloring. Put your favorite colored picture on the fridge. Play with stickers. Color outside with sidewalk chalk, Look up your favorite children's book, the earliest one you can remember, on Amazon, and order it. Or even just find it, and marvel at the images of its cover and inside pages. Nurture the tiny sweet girl within. And report back to Headquarters.

❖ CHAPTER 26 ❖

Queen or Slave Girl

"At every moment, a woman makes a choice: between the state of the queen and the state of the slave girl."
– Marianne Williamson

I remember the first time I read that line, in the life-changing pages of "A Woman's Worth."(A must-read, for any woman.)

It hit me in the gut like a punch in the stomach, took the wind out of me and cracked me open in a new way, because its truth resonated so deeply, so powerfully within me. It became a barometer by which I've measured my life and my choices, ever since.

There have been times, many times, that I have made choices aligned with that of the sad, lowly slave girl. Imprisoned by my own insecurities, uncertain of and without access to my own power. Boundaries a distant novelty. Without a map, without my inner GPS system activated, I've flailed around with an invisible sticker on my forehead: *"Love me? Please?"*

I've allowed, accepted and even encouraged others to treat me in a way that disempowered me, kept me enslaved by my own inability to demand respect. I've "kissed the creepy uncle" way too many times… (Did you have a creepy uncle that your parents forced you to be affectionate to, as a small girl, even if you didn't want to? I read somewhere that many of us are still metaphorically "kissing the creepy uncle", in our deeply-rooted addiction to 'being nice.')

I've allowed myself to engage in behaviors that while on the surface made me seem like 'the life of the party'... the wild one... the sexually progressive one... but were actually damaging acts of self-betrayal. 5Rythms creator, Gabrielle Roth says in her book "Sweat Your Prayers" (and I'm paraphrasing here...) "I've given my body to men I wouldn't have loaned my car to..." Yeah, Gabrielle. So have I.

I've flipped through the pages of unkind and dysfunctional magazines like Cosmo, while simultaneously feeling my self-esteem wither, my confidence dissolve, because I have never, nor will I *ever never*, look like those women. I've pored over the pages of sex tips so that I could learn how to be sexy, how to turn him on, how to make him beg for me, how to drive him crazy, how to keep him satisfied, how to 'cheat-proof' him. Yes, that was a real article title. As if that was ever, ever in our control.

I've believed the lies.

And sometimes I still do, for a minute.

But mostly, I remember the truth.

I know this:

That my worth and my power does not come from knowing how to please a man. It's way, way, WAY bigger and better than that.

That saying YES when I'd really rather say NO is an act self-betrayal, and I refuse to betray myself.

That MY pleasure, my happiness is my main priority.

That loving myself is the greatest gift I can give myself, AND my man.

That most "beauty" magazines are ugly. Poisonous. Damaging and full of lies.

That real sexual power comes not from 'driving him wild', 'cheat-proofing', or keeping him satisfied, but by being a woman in love with herself, who views sex as a vehicle for self-expression, connection and mutual pleasure.

That my body is my temple, and not up for grabs, in any way.

That I no longer have to "kiss the creepy uncle." Those days are over.

That when I slip into 'slave girl' mode by making one dishonoring choice, I can quickly jump right back into Queen status, by my next choice.

That I choose to own my power as a glorious and noble queen, reigning sovereign over the kingdom of me.

* * * *

❖ TRUTH

How, in your life, have you acted as slave girl? And how have you acted as queen? What do YOU know for sure, about your own queenly status? What promises can you make to yourself, to commit to a lifetime of sovereignty, over slavery?

❖ DARE

I dare you to consider one area where you have 'sold yourself out', where you have made disempowered choices... one relationship that brings out the lowly slave girl in you, drains you of your energy or saps you of your glory. Take one action, large or small, on behalf of your queenly status, toward that area. It's time. Share your action and let us know how it went in the Facebook Group!

❖ CHAPTER 27 ❖

This is What Love Looks Like

My teen daughter and I have started this fun tradition of writing love notes for each other with dry-erase markers on our shared bathroom mirror... things like *"Hey gorgeous!"* and *"You are beautiful!"* and *"I love you so much!"* and other sweet somethings.

Yesterday morning, I had the brilliant idea to draw a giant heart, so that when she looked in the mirror, the heart would frame her precious face. Underneath the heart, with an arrow pointing up at it, I wrote "This is what love looks like."

Except I didn't stop to think that *I, myself* would actually have to look at it.

In the middle of a deep blue funk.

With puffy allergy eyes that look like pillows.

After one very private peanut-butter cookie rampage.

Feeling fat.

And disgusting.

Needing a shower.

(Bad.)

And feeling like the absolute furthest thing from *"what love looks like."*

Yep. Later that night, forgetting I had drawn that, I went to use that sink. Puffy-eyed, shower-needing, low-self-esteem-feeling, in the middle of one helluva self-cruelty rendezvous, and was startled by my own words staring back at me, and that heart, that damned heart. I was feeling shameful and gross. *This is what love looks like?*

I don't think so.

PFFT... whatev.

I turned my head to look away while I washed my hands. I couldn't bear the truth of my own words. Not at that moment. Nope. No, thank you. After all, I wrote them for *her*, not me.

This is what love looks like.

It almost seemed like a taunt.

Yeah sure... with cookie crumbs on my décolletage...

This is what love looks like.

I can't even look.

This is what love looks like.

And suddenly, it wasn't my voice, but the voice of the Divine that I heard in my head...

This is what love looks like...

Even now, right now.

Not just when you're radiant and confident.

Not just when you're strong and bold.

Not just when you feel like light and love.

Even when you feel like dark and loathing.

Even when you're feeling the opposite of sacred or sexy.

Not just when you're feeling 'thin and in control.'

Even when you think you are a fuck-up.

This is what love looks like...

Because *you are love*.

And then... the voice asked a question.

"Now. Can you extend even just the tiniest bit of tenderness toward yourself, in this moment?"

Yes. I answered. Or at least I can try. And I turned toward my reflection, with love in my puffy, allergy eyes and extended Love toward myself. As is.

So now, I dare you, go look in the mirror, AS YOU ARE, right now, and extend a little tenderness toward yourself.

Because *you* are what love looks like, too.

* * * *

❖ TRUTH

When are you meanest to yourself? What are some of the most terrible things you say to yourself? What triggers those thoughts?

❖ DARE

The next time you are beating yourself up, I dare you to stop, mid-thought, if you can, and remind yourself that you are Divinity incarnate. That you are pure and magnificent love. That your beauty comes in your totality and that your totality includes every part, dark and light.

Next, ask yourself if you can possibly extend love yourself instead of the negative, cruel things you were saying. If you can, go ahead and extend that love to yourself, to the part of you that you were just bashing.

If your answer is no, you cannot, then ask for a higher love to love you through you. In other words, open yourself as a channel for a love bigger than your love, more perfect and accepting and let that love move through you to love that part of you that is hardest to love.

Do this as often as possible, and watch your capacity for self-kindness grow.

❖ PART THREE ❖

It's Good to be Queen:
*Reigning Sovereign
Over the Kingdom of You*

❖ CHAPTER 28 ❖

The Art of Being Blue

"Lower vibrating emotion is just information."
- Colette Baron-Reid

There was a time in my life when I was afraid of every 'negative' feeling, when I believed that feelings just 'happened' to us, that we were slaves to our thoughts and beliefs, that our job was to just surrender to whatever notion, mood or shitty feeling that set up camp in our consciousness.

While I DO still believe that *resistance* to our blue, grey or other feelings and moods can get us into trouble, I also believe that we have far more control over our moods, funks and feelings than we want to admit. That we are the boss of our mind, not the other way around, and that our worst, darkest, scariest moods and feelings are *little more than messengers*. As Collette says in the quote above: *information*.

So, the next time you find yourself in a nasty, deep-blue funk, ask yourself these questions:

- Do I want to be here?
- Do I need to be here?
- Am I ready to return to the light?

It's okay if you're NOT ready. Sometimes the healthiest thing to do with our funks is to roll around in them and feel them and wallow a spell. But, if you decide that you are ready to get out of the mud, begin to explore the information being offered to you by your funk.

Be aware, the scariest thing about doing this is that the information you discover may apply to areas of your life that you've been trying your *damnedest* to ignore, numb, or distract yourself from. In fact, it's likely that the funk IS THE PRODUCT of you trying your damnedest to ignore, numb or distract yourself from something.

The information may look like one or more of these babies...

- I really need to get out of this relationship...
- I am giving way more than I am getting back in this friendship...
- This job is killing me...
- I need to explore these old wounds and heal them once and for all....
- I've been sabotaging my success for far too long...
- I'm terrified of intimacy and would rather shut down than be vulnerable.

In other words, this exploration is not for wimps, but neither is a live fully lived. You may choose to explore these issues with a trusted friend, coach or therapist.

Either way, YOU ARE IN CHARGE, and whenever you're ready, *truly ready*, to commit to your joy, to bravely approach your demons, to claim sovereignty over your life, and make it beautiful- *whenever you're ready is the perfect time*. Really, it is.

The darkness is necessary but the light is always waiting for you.

* * * *

❖ TRUTH

When you are feeling funky, cranky or blue, what is typically the underlying message of your murk? Dare you speak it out loud? Or should that be our DARE?

❖ DARE

Confess your underlying truth, the one you most enjoy avoiding, to the Facebook Group. This dare requires great courage. Not for wimps. Do it... because you're not a wimp.

Write down on a piece of paper the following questions:

- Do I want to be here?
- Do I need to be here?
- Am I ready to return to the light?

Put in an envelope marked "To be opened in the midst of my next dark, cranky, crappy mood".

❖ CHAPTER 29 ❖

Just Your Everyday, Run-of-the-Mill Unspoken Terrors of Living

When my daughter was a little girl, she worried a lot. Tornadoes, death, the afterlife, war, stepping in dog poo, spider bites. You name it. I did the best I could to comfort her, to alleviate her worries, talk about odds and protection and precautions.

As she got older, and I'd run out of comforting things to say, and she understood playful sarcasm, I would tease in a sing-songy, June Cleaver voice "There, there, don't be afraid. Nothing bad *EVER* happens." It was a joke, sort of. A prayer, sort of. It was a way of admitting to one another that life is scary. Shit happens. People die. People can get hurt. People can hurt you.

Living is dangerous business. What else could I do but joke and laugh that "nothing bad *ever* happens"?

I've been a mom for 17 years now. And I realize now, from the moment I found out I was pregnant, in 1994, there is a special brand of fear that accompanies parenting that never goes away. It simply changes form.

When I was pregnant, I was afraid of something going wrong with the pregnancy. I was afraid of birth defects, of ripping, of losing her, of other unspeakable fears. When she was born, I was afraid of not feeding her enough, or too much, of diaper rash, of SIDS, of her being snatched, of her choking on spit-up, allergic reactions, colic, of her death.

As she grew, I was afraid of babysitters not being kind to her, of day care horrors and kidnapping and hospital emergencies. Then she went to school, and I was afraid of bullies, of playground injuries, lurking child molesters… and then there was high school and the fears transformed yet again… drugs, date rape, pregnancy, broken hearts, car accidents… it never ends.

Am I alone?

I think this shadowy, dark part of mothering (this also applies to simply 'living') rarely gets discussed.

We don't really speak of the terror that accompanies parenting. The heaviness that exists in accepting that anything awful, at any time, can happen, no matter how much we try to avoid or prevent it.

The possibility of loss… always there. The possibility of pain, of danger, never leaves.

We simply distract ourselves with the stuff of life, the day to day, the optimal experiences, the plans, the activities. But it's there, this terror, looming and quiet, ever-present.

We want to protect our babies, we want to protect ourselves, from pain, from loss, from suffering.

But we must go on living, imagining we have limitless tomorrows. As if *nothing bad ever happens* and we have all the time in the world. We inhale, we exhale, we pray. We hope, anyway. We live, anyway.

What other choice do we have?

* * * *

❖ TRUTH

What are your thoughts? What are your "favorite fears"? How do you deal with the looming, shadowy terror of everyday life? Where do you find balance between dark and light? Living and hiding? Trusting and fearing? Do tell.

❖ DARE

Sometimes simply stating our fears out loud can diminish their dark, shadowy potency. They can even seem silly in the light of day, once we claim them and dare to name them. With a trusted friend, or in the Truth or Dare Facebook Group, list your fears, one by one. Name them, claim them, and then see if they don't slip down a couple notches on your scale of importance or magnitude.

❖ CHAPTER 30 ❖

Hitting Bottom

"The hardest part of hitting bottom is the descent. Once you land, little lights appear. You make your way toward them."
- Lauren Slater

What does "hitting bottom" look like to you? What does it feel like?

We humans spend so much of our lives avoiding pain, rejection and discomfort at all costs. We concoct all kinds of elaborate ways to avoid them... addictions, compulsions, distractions, diversions in our misguided attempts to numb/hide/escape/anesthetize. Yet the game cannot go on forever, and eventually we fall on our proverbial faces.

The secrets come out. The jig is up. The lights are on. *There's no where left to hide.*

There's it is- the gift, I think, in hitting bottom: *There's no where left to hide.*

Even if that bottom is as 'minor' as a carb hangover after a potato chip binge that leaves you deep in a pool of self-loathing and shame. Our rock bottoms, whatever they may be, invite us out from hiding. And there's nothing liberating about shame or self-sabotage. Come down from your lonely fortress, that you've built brick by brick, choice by choice, self-betrayal by self-betrayal. Your fortress of protection is really a prison in disguise.

What if your next rock bottom was an invitation from your Highest, most Magnificent Self to change? To turn in your battered 'tools of the trade'... isolation, secrets, obsessions, self-destructive behaviors... all at one time seemingly smart tactics for survival. Tools that now, as your rock bottom tells you, *obsolete in the light of your emerging Self.*

May your (and my) next rock bottom offer us those little lights... instead of shaming us or immersing us in regret or self-debasement, may it show us *another way*, and lead us to deep healing and profound self-love, as we step into the Light. We may squint for the brightness, and the shadows may try to coax us back into their safety. But it's from the bottom that we make our way toward the light most earnestly.

* * * *

❖ TRUTH

Where does your shame live? Are you willing and ready to release it, and its hold on you, once and for all? What has it cost you? Share your shame, courageously and openly, with the Facebook group, or in your journal. Where in your life are you being invited to heal?

❖ DARE

Take one courageous action that will help dismantle the fortress of protection that is no longer serving you. If it means coming clean of a secret that has long held you bound, find a trusted friend to confess to, or create a postcard of your secret and send it to postsecret.com, an anonymous secret-sharing community. Make amends with someone you have wronged. Let yourself off the hook. Throw away momentos that make you feel bad about yourself. Commit to growth. Forgive yourself.

❖ CHAPTER 31 ❖

Your Resistance Isn't Working

*"The heart is abloom
Shoots up through the stony ground…"*
-U2 "Beautiful Day"

When truth comes, when light returns, when insight moves from head to heart, and becomes embodied, healing begins.

Your resistance isn't working. It only causes more pain.

Melt into your pain, sink into it, like rain into soil, explore it, breathe into it.

Hear it.

It started as a whisper so many years ago, but you did not listen. Are you ready now to hear? Now that it is screaming. It is crying, begging for you to heed, to change, to let go.

When what was stony within you begins to crack open, and a bud pushes through, longing to bloom, you know you are on your path to healing.

You lament… *"If this pain went away, THEN I could do what I came here to do. THEN I could do what I need to do. I have work to do. I could get this pain out of the way, and get back on my path…"*

What if the pain IS the way, for now? What if this pain IS the path, for now? What if it IS your work, what you need to do, what you came here to do, for now?

How might that change your approach? The way you experience it? The way you 'handle' this pain?

It's time for a new approach. One that involves love, and surrender. One that listens and obeys. One that chooses according to truth and does not lie. An approach that moves through with curiosity and respect, instead of stony resistance.

Is it time for the bloom to push through the stony ground? It is for me.

May you experience relief from your pain by surrendering to it, investigating it, and melting into it.

Your resistance isn't working, either, I bet.

* * * *

❖ TRUTH

What have you been resisting? What pain have you been working hard to avoid? What do you feel is in the way of the life you would rather be living?

❖ DARE

Surrender to what is. Can you love this experience? Can you simply love this area of your life that you have been resisting? If you cannot find a way to love it, allow yourself to become a channel of love from a divine source, whatever that may mean for you. Allow your prayer to be *Love this through me,* if you cannot find love in your own heart for your pain. Instead of considering this to be in your way, open to the idea that perhaps instead, *it is the way.* Practice sending love to this area of your life daily, for seven days, and notice the transformation.

❖ CHAPTER 32 ❖

Top-Secret Strategy for Funk Removal

Recognize any of these strategies for escaping feelings?

- avoidance
- distraction
- obsession
- addiction
- numbing
- blaming
- bailing

I've rolled around with all of them myself, as clever ways of escaping the feelings I just didn't want to feel.

Through years of lots and lots of personal work, I've learned a LOT about navigating my grey days, the fine art of being blue, how to juice a funk, and masterfully riding my sometimes precarious roller coaster of emotions.

I've recently had some great shifts by changing my diet. I had no idea how much the foods I'd been eating were influencing my emotions. I'm enjoying more consistent joy and contentment, instead of the intense emotional highs and lows my flour and sugar addiction provided.

I know how to allow my feelings to move through me.

I'm learning how to let my 'lower' emotions (the ones I don't like) *inform* me, invite me to what I most need in that moment... Clarity. Action. Compassion. Stillness. Forgiveness.

I am becoming an expert of being the *ocean*, and not the boat. Instead of letting my emotions knock me around, (or any other unlucky soul who might happen to step in my pile o' funk...) I am becoming adept at being spacious enough for any emotion, being a safe place for every feeling.

It's strange to me when people say things to me like "you're always just so happy all the time!"

I wonder how or why they've one-dimensionalized me. *Have they read my last Facebook post?* I ponder. Yes, my natural disposition is joy, and I do experience it daily, most of the time. But then there's the funk. The funkytown blechy funkiness funkville funk.

I do step out of my joy (or *fall* out, sometimes) for a number of reasons, like we all do. I posted once as a status *"Can't decide if I'm eh, meh, blah or blech."* (I think I was all four.)

The feeling pissy for no-good-reason, being scared or slipping down the well of old stories and poor-me crap that comes out of nowhere sometimes. Shuts me down. Folds me up. Kinks the flow. Plucks me out of delight and wonder and ease.

And sometimes, I just don't want to waste my time there. I'm not in the mood for my bad mood. *Give me back my joy. Where's my happy place? Where'd I put my bliss? I know I left it around here somewhere...*

Ya feel me?

I've got a great strategy I want to share with you, for YOUR funky "meh" moods... you know what I mean. The indifference, frustration, blechy blahs that don't seem to be doing anything except stealing your joy. For the next time you're not in the mood for your bad mood.

Next time you are in your own crappy mood and you really want to step back into joy, you can do it in 20 minutes or less.

Here's the technique:

Initiate a love campaign. A love storm. A love blitz.

I do it on Facebook, (cuz that's my neighborhood, where I hang out) but you can do it by phone, by mail, by email, by text... whatever.

Everyone who steps into your path gets at least one (if not two or three or ten) sentences about how wonderful they are. What you love about them, how you appreciate their presence in your life. How beautiful they are to you. How important they are to the world. Notice their divinity. Acknowledge their radiance. Lift them up.

Don't fake it. Speak truth from the heart. And watch the miracle happen. (Or science. Same thing.)

Do this several times in a row. Slam them with love.

Oxytocin and endorphins will begin to pump through your system. You will feel energized. Your mood will begin to shift. You may even feel giddy, overjoyed, even *dizzy*, when dispensing large amounts of love.

Mmmm yeah, you're love-drunk, baby.

Be a lover to everyone who shows up. Or even the ones who don't.

Surprise someone with your love.

Tickle fancies.

Stroke egos.

Fill hearts with joy.

Build up.

Douse self-doubt.

Stoke someone's soul fire.

The ripple effects are enormous, and what might have started out as a "selfish" way to get out of a blue funk will do so much more. Because we all know that what the world needs now is love, sweet love.

And love will save the day.

You'll be surprised how often you'll hear things like *"You don't know how much I needed to hear that."* The universe is an intricate tapestry of spoken and unspoken prayers, and the subsequent responses. BE a subsequent response.

Show up for love.

Enlist.

Recruit.

Become a Certified Love Administrator.

Be a soldier in the Cosmic Love Army.

Yummy-yummy-yummmmy...

Now what was that I was cranky about, again?

* * * *

❖ TRUTH

How do you respond to the funk? That blue-grey unhappy sticky place that rocks you off of your center. Do you lash out at co-workers? Withdraw, fold inward, become anti-social? Scream at the kids, avoid physical affection with your partner? What is your 'funk-style'? Do share.

❖ DARE

Initiate your own personal Love Campaign. For the next week, go out of your way to express love, affection, cheer, compliments, praise, acknowledgments, kindness on a daily basis to your intimates and your acquaintances. Total strangers. Spread the love. Pay special attention to how these acts make you feel. Report back to Headquarters with your tales!

❖ CHAPTER 33 ❖

Good Grief

"The only way out is through..."

Becca, one of my closest friends and I are talking about a party she was at over the weekend and how it became, for her, quite the un-party, when a certain ex-boyfriend showed up, we'll call him Dick.

Becca went on dancing, laughing, having a great time, perhaps a little too hard, for that extra 'see-I'm-totally-fine-without-your-dumb-ass' affect, and they did not say hi to one another.

"And so of course, afterward," she says with a certain degree of self-loathing. 'like an idiot, I kept waiting for him to call me, to text me, something, because no doubt seeing me stirred up his feelings, made him realize what a fool he'd been, made him miss me...' there was no call. There was no text. She felt stupid. Mad at herself for caring. For still having emotions wrapped up and tangled in the situation that seeing him at the party triggered for her . Feelings she did not want to have.

"I just want to be done with it. So this morning I scheduled a session with an energy worker because obviously I still have some connection. I want it cut, once and for all..."

I've been thinking about Becca since, about our conversation, about cutting the cord, and I want to save her a hundred dollars by giving her permission to *simply grieve...*

Ugh, grief. Perhaps the shittiest of all emotions, the one we go to all kinds of crazy, creative ways to avoid feeling, we'd love to skip it all together, because it sucks, but we can't, so even when we think we do, grief just hides out, in our body, in our hearts, in our subconscious, like a cancer, who knows, maybe even literally becoming a cancer, or a nervous breakdown, or sleeplessness, or misplaced (usually self-directed) loathing, or headaches, or back pain, or drug addiction, or compulsive eating, or shoplifting, or promiscuity, or… a million other things. It finds a way to express itself, somehow. Grief unexpressed, pain and heartbreak unfelt, do not just dissipate into the ether.

Because Becca is like me, and maybe you, a "Big-Strong-Girl", she plowed through her pain and heartbreak like a big-strong-girl does, but my Spidery-senses are telling me she hasn't really given her sweet, injured heart the time and space it needed… to be broken. To be wounded. To heal.

Have you ever fallen, say, in public? Like I'm talking you lose your balance and just take a dive and hit the ground? Most likely, in front of a large number of people, who then are inspired to applaud, laugh awkwardly, or, if it's a really good dive, gasp and wince, crying out "OOOH…. that had to hurt!" If you are like me, you are brave and tough and you laugh ha-ha-ha, even though it hurts and your knees and the palms of your hands are stinging, throbbing, you are a big-strong-girl!

You jump back up quickly, dust yourself off, to show the world just how Okay you truly are, no-I'm-fine, really, smiling it off, not just *pretending* you are fine, but maybe even *thinking* you are fine, not even realizing your own pain, only to realize hours later, like when you pull down your jeans to pee, your knees are all banged up, bruised and bleeding, under your jeans. And THEN- that's when it starts to hurt.

I think that's what seeing Dick at the party was like for Becca. She felt fine, "look how fine she is!" Dancing, laughing, having a great old time, and then, bam! She sees his dumb-ass, it's like pulling down her tough-girl jeans, suddenly seeing the bruise, the blood, and not surprisingly, feeling the pain.

I have another friend, Daisy, who spent a butt-load of money on a private session with a shamanic healer after her painful break-up with her jackass boyfriend, who we'll call Jack, with some powerful ritual, and the healer cut the ties, snip snip, no more connection and after the session she was high as kite on healing energy, glowing, luminescent and healed, hallelujah. It's done, she gushed. Super shaman man cut the ties and it's done.

And for a few days she was great, until she was going through some forgotten piles of junk mail and papers and found a take-out menu from 'That's Amore', they had ordered from two weeks before he dumped her, when she thought things were just great and that he might possibly be The Love of Her Life, and she had ordered the chicken parmesan and he the baked lasagna and they had bloated carb-crash sex afterward, but it was great, and all of a sudden, she is sobbing on her living room floor, shaman man lied, the feelings are still there, there are still ties.

And I told her and I'll tell you, sweet reader: a ritual is great. Important, no doubt. In fact, I am firmly rooted in the belief that rituals need to be more a part of our lives, for endings, for beginnings, for heartbreak, for letting go, for holding on when it seems like there's nothing to hold onto. Rituals can help us heal, make for tidier incisions, cleaner stitches when we are dealing with an open wound, but guess what?

We don't get to skip the grief.

No shaman, no ritual, no energy worker, no one, regardless of how gifted they are or how much you pay them can heal you from grief. *It is the grief itself that heals* you.

Why are we so afraid of grief? We fear being swallowed, eaten alive by it, we're afraid if we go in we will never come out. But amazingly, and I am more sure about this than I may be anything else in the whole world, that it isn't until we experience our feelings completely that they can finally heal. And they do. They will. It is guaranteed.

We are bigger than our grief, no matter how big it may feel. How can something we hold inside of us, smaller than us, swallow us? There are no shortcuts through the darkness, no secret passageways that we can purchase by the session, by the hit, the book, the fix. The only fix is allowing.

"You are not broken. You are simply unfinished." – Dawna Markova

I believe that grief unexpressed, unprocessed, often hides out in the body. In fact, I've experienced this, firsthand.

The first time I was confronted with this theory, I was on the table at my Chiropractor's, on my back and she was working on me. She seemed focused on one particular area, the area where I was having a lot of pain, the pelvic and hip area. Dr. Jessica practiced a form of Chiropractic called Network Care, which is much gentler and more intuitive than typical chiropractic. There is no cracking or popping, all touch is gentle. She held my left leg and bent it upward and began stirring it in a circular motion. A strange feeling began to well up in that area and began to move up my body like a huge wave. I felt incredibly sad.

The motion she was making seemed to actually be loosening something emotional inside that area and she continued to stir up the big pot of whatever she was loosening, using my hip joint as a big mixing spoon. Suddenly, out of nowhere, I was sobbing. Uncontrollably sobbing. Waves of sadness washed up my body and all I could do was cry. I felt embarrassed and tried to stop and tried to apologize through snot-filled gasps for air.

"I don't even know why I'm crying!" I snorted. She nodded warmly and continued to work. After the session, Dr. Jessica told me she had found a huge block in my root chakra. I, knowing nothing at that time about such things, asked her what the root chakra related to. "Security. Home. Safety." She answered. Ah, yes. I thought. Pay dirt.

On my way home from her office, I stopped at a book store and bought a guide to chakra healing. The block in my root chakra made perfect sense, considering the home I grew up in, the things I struggled with currently and also the physical pain in my right hip I had been suffering from for nearly two years.

The second time it happened, I was enjoying (and I mean enjoying) my very first Thai massage. Thai massage, like most things, is better experienced than explained, but to give you an idea, it is done on the floor. The massage therapist uses her whole body- legs, chest, her weight, to stretch and move the client. There is lot of large motor motion in a Thai massage and again, as the therapist worked on my left side, that same area, a stirring began to well up in my left hip and I began to feel immersed in a deep and profound sadness. There was nothing to be sad about, I thought, but I struggled not to break down. That would be so embarrassing, my Inner Judge chastised me for thinking about having a meltdown during a massage. Of all places! It's supposed to feel good. It's not supposed to make you cry.

I struggled with this urge as it continued to well up in me, tried to stifle the tears, I tried hard to stay composed, but it was taking more energy *not* to cry and eventually I just gave in to the sadness. As I had done with the Chiropractor, I was quick to explain that I didn't know why I was crying. *I just feel so sad,* I sobbed. She stayed with me and breathed with me and let me cry as much as I needed to. You're safe, I could almost hear her saying out loud.

On the way home from my massage I thought about what I had felt, how the sadness had no particular story attached to it, nothing specific I could point at and say "and THAT'S why I'm crying." And I didn't really want to attach a story to it. The story, at this point, was irrelevant. The fact of the matter was (and is) the emotions that I did not allow myself to fully experience whenever the situation had originally occurred did not just dissolve into the air. Those feelings had just been stored- hidden in some nook or cranny in my body. After repeated sessions, it was clear to me that I had stored a great deal of sadness in my hips, as if there were pockets there, like a pair of jeans. "No. I can't feel this right now." I had unconsciously decided. For whatever reasons, denial, avoidance, self-protection, and since what is not expressed is repressed, I tucked that pain in the pocket's of my soul's jeans like chewed gum, and now, I was cleaning out the pockets and finding all this yucky, sticky stuff that had lost its original form, but still had its ingredients and was making a mess.

There would be two similar instances in which this sadness would come up during bodywork, once during a Shamanic healing session and once during a Reiki session. And again I am told there is "damage" to my root chakra.

I couldn't believe that all my healing work, all of these sessions, all of that sobbing and sadness that I had finally allowed to move through my body, I was still blocked in my freakin' root chakra.

I remember as a teenager, one hot summer day I had stepped on a pin out in front while hanging out. Instead of cleaning and covering the puncture, I continued to walk around barefoot. Soon I found myself with a severely infected foot. It looked like a balloon, swelled up ten times its original size, it was excruciatingly painful and I couldn't walk on it at all.

During that time, a visiting faith healer came to my church for revival meetings and healing services. Brother Razzle Dazzle had all the sleek and smooth charisma you might expect of a traveling faith healer and after each sermon, all the sick and wounded people were invited to the altar to be healed. I hobbled to the altar, my balloon foot so inflamed that I couldn't even let it touch the floor without crying out in pain. But I believed in the power of prayer and in miracles.

Brother Razzle Dazzle placed his hands on me and prayed and it was amazing. Miraculously and instantly, I could walk on my foot. While it still looked the same, like a soccer ball with toes, it no longer hurt. I had been healed. I walked back to my seat, using both feet, minus the limp, hands raised in the air, praising God for magically healing my foot.

Hours later though, after the endorphin rush had worn off, the pain returned with a vengeance, the swelling worsened and now I had a fever. It was time for the hospital. My failure to be healed was so disappointing and disheartening, and while I questioned the Faith Healer's abilities, mostly I blamed it on myself, for not having strong enough faith.

I am reminded of the foot healing now, and it all becomes a little clearer to me. The only true failures, whether we think its us failing or God failing us, happens when our containers are too small and limited. When we put deadlines on our discomfort, nurturing some silly notions of a completely pain-free existence. As if we could just bypass the suffering, if we just prayed hard enough, hired some healer, took the workshop.

I found it disappointing that in spite of all of my efforts, all of the intense and dramatic experiences I had experienced to clear my root chakra and to heal from whatever traumatic pain and sadness I had stored in that region, I was still blocked. I still had not received my miracle. I had lots of false 'breakthroughs' but when it was all said and done, I was still in physical pain and my chakra was still blocked.

Using my uncanny ability to twist things around so that I can feel bad about myself, I had translated this into: *I am still damaged. I am still broken. Fix me.* (I'll pay you.)

We look for a miracle, but we don't give that miracle any room to be whatever shape it may be. We want things to work out but our definitions of "working out" are thin and one dimensional.

It's as if we think we have that ONE answer to what "working out" should look like, and when we fail to see that exact version, we claim we didn't receive the miracle, or things didn't "work out."

What if my chakra was meant to stay blocked so that I could practice self-acceptance, or so that I can tell the story and one other person might feel validated who had previously felt flawed or damaged?

What if my body was healing at its own natural pace, instead of the instant-healing I kept looking for in healers and gurus? What if I could learn to just be with what is, blocked chakra and all, and love myself through it?

What if instead of looking for a miracle limited by my small thinking ("hey God: a miracle looks like this") I instead sought the miracles in the situation as is? What if i allowed myself to simply journey through my suffering, to see what awaits me on the other side?

I'm learning how to do life like that, and it starts with feeling all of my feelings and not avoiding the crappy ones when they show up. We want to skip the suffering. We want to avoid the pain. But truly, the only way out is through.

I implore you, in whatever hidden recesses your grief or pain might be tucked into, to experiment with allowing it to show up when it will, to not be afraid when it turns you inside out, to allow yourself space and time to grieve.

How much time? As much time as it takes.

How much space? As much space as it wants.

You won't get swallowed up. You won't. Be easy and gentle with yourself and know that when pain is triggered, it's not a bad thing.

You are not flawed, not broken or damaged. Simply and beautifully real and human. Grief and sadness are not something to avoid, but to travel through, finding richness and wholeness and the depth that only experiencing life in all of its slippery sloppiness and sharp jagged corners can provide.

The healing happens naturally, through the pain itself. It is the way through.

You dishonor yourself by denying your experience of pain. When you acknowledge whatever's there, and allowing yourself to feel it fully, healing happens.

If there is a secret passageway, this is it: allowing yourself to feel what needs to be felt to heal.

* * * *

❖ TRUTH

What painful area of your life seems to keep returning, in spite of your best efforts to heal, complete, or be done with?

❖ DARE

I dare you to enter your grief. Instead of avoiding it, next time it shows up, simply enter it. Let it move through you. Cry if you need to cry. Feel what you need to feel.

❖ CHAPTER 34 ❖

Stillness

"Stand still. The forest knows where you are."
– Mary A. Hall

I heard this on an internet program audio replay one morning, and of course, like so many things I read or hear, it came at the perfect time, in the perfect moment, a little miracle, a mini-rescue.

I was getting ready to take a month off to focus on healing and restoring my body. The decision to stop might have been one of the most radical act of self-care I've ever done. Never mind 'might be'. It was.

As a kid, did you ever wander away from the grown-ups, and suddenly find yourself lost? In the woods, at an amusement park, at the mall? And the more you bounced around trying to find your way, the more lost you got? And the panic starts to set in, and you cry. And when you stop wandering to cry, and just stand still, someone magically comes to help you. Mall security. A forest ranger. Your mom finds you. First she hugs you, then she scolds you: *Don't you ever wander off like that again!* You're relieved, and safe.

Remember this, and I will remember it, too: when you are hurting, confused or lost there is *always* something much bigger and wiser holding you, supporting you. *The forest knows where you are.* The trees are whispering to you their secrets. But to hear them, you must stand still.

That's what I did this month. Deeply exploring stillness, for the first time ever, really. And yeah, I'll admit, it was scary. It's interesting to see and feel the things that rise to the surface when there is nothing to distract or busy myself with. Some dark stuff. Some important stuff. Some shadowy, sticky stuff. It's no wonder I'm so much more comfortable moving around all the time. (You should see the tangled mess of sheets in my bed every morning. I'm even 'busy' when I sleep.)

* * * *

❖ TRUTH

How do you know when it's time to stand still? When to stop? Does stillness come easy for you? Are you able to trust in the wisdom of the forest, whatever the forest may symbolize for you? What do you do when you don't know what to do?

In your journal or in the Living Truth or Dare Facebook Group, speak your Truth.

❖ DARE

What would happen if you just stood still? If you stopped your doing, and just experienced being.

I dare you to stop. For half an hour, three hours, maybe for a day, a week. Commit to your time off in your journal or the private Facebook Group. Stop, sit. Lay. And do absolutely nothing.

❖ CHAPTER 35 ❖

You Say Self-Centered As If It's a Bad Thing

I've grown weary of this idea that being anything other than self-centered is good. The term itself, self-centered, is used to describe our villains, our antagonists. It's lumped up there (or down there) with terms like narcissistic, conceited, self-absorbed and vain.

What if we shifted that? What if we took the literal interpretation of the phrase as its new, improved definition?

Self-centered: centered in self.

For where else would we rather be centered? Who else would we rather have as our centers?

Who decided that being self-centered is a bad thing?

I declare, in my own personal commitment to radical self-care that I deliberately embrace the concept of self-centeredness. I use 'self-centeredness' as a barometer to measure whether or not a certain activity, relationship or choice brings me to my center, (my self's center...) or diverts me from my center.

As someone who is self-centered, I will find myself making choices based on the joy they bring, or based on my heart's truest desires. I find myself dancing more, laughing more, loving more. Expressing more. Allowing more. Inviting more. Savoring more. That's what someone who is self-centered does.

I choose to radiate a strong sense of self. Yeah, I'm self-centered. And I'm okay with it!

I am not you-centered. I am not they-centered, he-centered, she-centered. I am self-centered. Because as far as I can see, that's the best place to be.

* * * *

❖ TRUTH

Make a list of things a "self-centered" person does. Don't worry about placing judgment, right-or-wrongs on the items. Just list. For example:

A self-centered person...

- Divorces her husband
- Takes long hot baths, every day
- Vacations alone
- Calls in sick when she feels like it
- Screens her phone calls

❖ DARE

Which of the items on your list appeal to you? Tickle you? Pull you? Choose one item and either do it, or begin planning to do it. Share your self-centered decisions in the Facebook group, if you dare.

❖ CHAPTER 36 ❖

Trust Your Own Importance

I've gotten into this deliciously wonderful habit of buying fresh flowers for myself and it's been one of my better habits, I must say.

The other day I was in the grocery store, eyeing the floral offerings, and a particular bouquet of miniature roses caught my eye. They looked like fire– a gorgeous blend of orange, fuchsia, yellow and red, each miniature rose painted with exquisite detail. The bouquet was ten bucks. And I was "broke"- translation- I had "no business" buying anything other than the "bare necessities."

It felt frivolous, selfish... silly.

I put the roses back and thought... when I can afford them, Imma come back...

But the roses wouldn't leave me alone. I thought about them while picking up my bare necessities, and eventually a clear voice came to me, through my heart, and said:

Beauty is a necessity.

Roses make you happy.

Romance yourself.

I went back to the floral department, grabbed the roses and instantly felt my heart open up with glee. All the way home, I kept thinking,

"I am someone who acknowledges her desires.

I am someone who trusts her own importance. I am worth it…

I am someone who buys herself roses."

It was a small, inexpensive indulgence, and although some might think it wasn't financially responsible of me, it wasn't like a ten-dollar bouquet would put me in the poor house.

And ohhhhh, those roses! Within two days or so, dozens of tiny buds opened and bloomed loudly and proudly, to me and for me. A gift I savored for more than a week. Never for one second did that feel like a waste of money. I enjoyed the HELL out of these roses.

The romantic experience of loving myself enough and walking in to my home over and over again that week and a half to see them there, to enjoy them all over again, was worth every red cent.

* * * *

❖ TRUTH

What small indulgence have you been denying yourself?

Would anything "bad" happen if you just went and did it/bought it/ate it/gave it/picked it/said it/released it/grabbed it/touched it/loved it?

I doubt it.

And what would be your reward?

❖ DARE

Romance yourself in one small way today. And maybe an even bigger way, come tomorrow…

❖ CHAPTER 37 ❖

Let Yourself Off the Hook

There is a very famous book that has a reputation of being a sort of "sacred text" when it comes to esoteric and metaphysical spirituality, called "Seat of the Soul" by Gary Zukav.

Over the years, I've tried to read this book at least five times.

I have bought it and then resold it to the local used bookstore just as many times.

I have this book. Spiritual people love this book. *I'm spiritual people.* Why don't I love this book? wanted so badly to dive into its pages. So many people I know have loved this book. *Oprah* loves his books.

Although I haven't verbalized this, or even conceptualized it, til now, it was as if I was asking, without words, *"What's wrong with me, that I don't love this book?"*

The first couple times, I thought "maybe I'm just not ready for the information." I promised myself I'd return to it, in perfect time. Like later... when I was deeper. More holy. Smarter. Wiser.

I'd try again a couple years later, pushing through the same first couple chapters like I was preparing for some test. A spirituality test. *"Are You Spiritual Enough?"* Again, I'd hit the wall: *"I'm just not digging this book."* It's certainly not the book. It must be me.

Do you ever find yourself doing certain things, reading certain books, participating in certain activities because you think that's what "blank" people are supposed to do... spiritual people... good people... smart people... worthy people... holy people... sexy people... whatever...

Chanting at kirtan because that's what ecstatic spiritual people do?

Sitting in church because that's what good Christians do?

Sitting in the dark trying to meditate because that's what good Buddhists do?

Allowing someone you're not attracted to in the least to make advances on you, because that's what flirty people do?

I've done all of the above, at some point in my life, and sometimes, truth be told, I'm going through the motions, not because I was hungry for it. But because that's what I thought I "should" do. I was trying to fit into a "notion" of who I thought I should be, instead of just being who I really, truly was.

I saw Gary Zukav interviewed by Oprah a couple weeks ago. I LOVED what he had to say. Everything that came out of his mouth resonated with me. *I'm buying the book again*, I told myself. *I think I'm ready now.*

I bought it, I snuggled down to read it. It bored me to tears.

And then I made a realization. It's not the information that doesn't resonate. It's the delivery. I thought of my favorite authors, Marianne Williamson, Mark Nepo, Oriah, Dawna Markova, and I thought about how much I love their poetic, loving, lyrical way of delivering spiritual messages. I like spiritual writing that reads like poetry. Zukav's writing style is much more pragmatic, matter-of-fact, almost scientific. It doesn't sing to me like Rumi. It doesn't embrace me like Nepo. And I don't have to read it.

Truth of the matter is, I look to books to do more than inform me. I want to be seduced. I wanted to be made love to by words. I want to savor delicious phrases, sometimes reading them over and over because the way they are organized is scrumptious and satisfying and lush and gorgeous.

Maybe someday I will pick up Seat of the Soul and devour it. Maybe I won't. I'm not going to judge myself anymore about it. I'm not going to deem myself more or less spiritual, intelligent or anything, just because a guy who's appeared on Oprah over thirty times doesn't have a writing style that grabs me.

He's okay, I'm okay.

And it's all okay. I'm letting myself off the hook.

Can you let yourself off the hook today, with some 'should' that just ain't clicking for ya? Come on, I dare you. It feels pretty good.

* * * *

❖ TRUTH

What's one thing you've judged yourself about that you've wanted to do, or read or practice, that for whatever reason, just hasn't clicked for you?

❖ DARE

I dare you to let it go. For now, remove it from your list of shoulds and let yourself off the hook. Instead, experiment with something else. See how that goes, instead.

❖ CHAPTER 38 ❖

Do Nothing

"Rest is not idleness, and to lie sometimes on the grass on a summer day listening to the murmur of water, or watching the clouds float across the sky, is hardly a waste of time."
- Sir John Lubbock

Where and when and how did we learn the lie that 'doing nothing' was a bad thing? As cliché as this term has become, we are human beings, not human DOINGS, yet we place so much importance on being busy, as if our worth is in direct correlation to our overwhelm. I'm tired of that.

I've been dealing with an unpredictable and frustrating chronic pain situation, one that literally has me flat on my back at times. I've had a lot of time lately to think about this doing nothing concept... Sometimes, I've even been doing it. Nothing. No book, no TV, no radio show, no computer. Just nothingness and me. And it's awkward. I'm not very used to spending time with nothing, doing nothing...

I lay, I close my eyes, I nudge myself toward the doing nothingness that feels like an indulgent treat, one that I deserve.

I close my eyes, I think, I pray, I make lists in my mind... and then I remind myself that there I go again... doing.

It's a hard habit to break, yet I'm committed to learning how. And I think my healing journey depends on it. I'm really good at doing. Can I become an expert at not-doing?

* * * *

❖ TRUTH

What about you? When was the last time you did nothing- absolutely nothing? Do you have feelings of guilt when you lay around doing nothing? What lessons did you learn growing up about resting, about stopping? Things like "idle hands are the devil's playground"? What would your life be like with less doing and more being? Do you meditate? I want to hear from you.

In your journal or in the Living Truth or Dare Facebook Group, speak your Truth.

❖ DARE

Right now, go to your calendar and schedule 3 'Do nothing days' over the next three months- one Do Nothing Day per month. And then, when those days come, do nothing. Give yourself permission to stay in bed all day, watch bad TV, stay in your PJs, hell… you can even skip brushing your teeth if you want to really maximize the do-nothing challenge. Post your chosen dates in the Facebook Group for accountability.

❖ PART FOUR ❖

Fully, Wildly, Passionately

Dare to live, really live

❖ CHAPTER 39 ❖

This is Why I Believe in Miracles: Because I AM One.

When I was thirteen, I nearly succeeded at killing myself. For all intents and purposes, it should have worked. I had enough pills to do it. A colorful combo of 80+ pills, including sedatives, pain relievers and whatever else I could secretly pilfer. I'd been collecting them for weeks. A couple here, a couple there… so no one would notice them missing.

Then why was it when I was taking them all, and dropped one particular pill, I picked it up, saw it was dusty and threw it back down?

Why was it when I got home after taking all the pills (not having died on the bus, like I'd planned) crabby with a splitting headache, wanting more than anything to lay down in my room and die, my mother made me lay on the couch in the living room so I could let her know when the carpet cleaners arrived? I argued so hard with her. She didn't relent. So on the couch I threw myself. I was unconscious by the time the carpet cleaners arrived.

Why was it, as I hung to life with the help of machines, as the doctors gave a bleak prognosis of complete recovery to my parents, that within a day or so I was fully recovered, with no liver, heart or brain damage, as they had predicted?

The doctor later told us how lucky I was. That one more little orange pill would have killed me.

And if I had gone to my room and fallen unconscious, instead of on the couch, no one would have noticed for hours and I would have died.

Because I was meant to live. Because I am a miracle.

It didn't take me long to realize this. I knew then that no matter how painful life could get, there was always hope for tomorrow. That things changed. That there was a God looking out for me. That I was not allowed to squander my life away, wishing I was dead.

Miracles come in all shapes and sizes. As I share in the interview, sometimes a miracle is as subtle as acceptance. A simple shift in consciousness. Forgiveness. Letting go. Surrender. Healing. A ladybug landing on your hand, just as you were sinking into despair. A job interview just in time. A phone call. A smile from a stranger at the perfect moment.

But sometimes, they are huge. Where you 'shoulda' died, but you didn't.

And I have never forgotten my big miracle. Or that my life itself is nothing short of miraculous.

* * * *

❖ TRUTH

Make a list of miracles that you have seen, heard about or experienced first-hand. Go beyond the earth-shattering, and consider the miracles that we take for granted, every day.

❖ DARE

Ask for a miracle.

❖ CHAPTER 40 ❖

For Angels and Lovers

"Women need to be in love: with themselves, with a man, with a child, with a project, with a job, with their country, with the planet and most important- with life itself. Women in love are closer to enlightenment. For angels and lovers, everything sparkles."
– Marianne Williamson

I've learned something about myself over the years and it's become a guiding principle in my life.

Without passion to fuel any endeavor, project or relationship, I find it near impossible to stay invested- emotionally or energetically.

Sure, I can go through the motions, squeezing out paltry efforts and less than enthusiastic results, but there's no juice. It's no fun. If it doesn't light my fire, I'm not really interested.

On the other hand... when I AM passionate about an endeavor, project or relationship, I am energized, engaged and excited. Sure, I may face challenges or days that feel more struggly than blissy... but even so, when I can reconnect to my passion for what I'm involved in, I shine. I rock. I roll. I kick ass. And that juice, that energy seeps into *every other area* in my life.

Am I passionate about taking out the garbage? Hell no. But when I am *lit from within* for a hot, passion-fueled project or situation in my life, I can take out the garbage with a spring in my step. And get back to 'work' which seems more like fun, like pleasure.

What pleases you? What lights you up? What are you wildly in love with in your life? As Marianne implies above, it's not so important WHAT or WHO you're in love with.

It matters more that you simply love *something* wildly.

Anything. Be a lover. Because for angels and lovers, everything sparkles. YUM.

* * * *

❖ TRUTH

What are you most passionate about? What are you in love with. Write in your journal, or share in the Facebook group some of the things you love wildly.

❖ DARE

Choose one item from your list that you seem to have gotten away from. We all have those passions that we devote so little time to. What small action can you take to return yourself to your passion? Can you call the local community college and find out about oil painting class? Can you devote yourself to an afternoon of writing? Can you make a date to see that long-lost friend that you love so dearly, but see so rarely? Take action. Return to your passion.

"It's the soul's duty to be loyal to its own desires. It must abandon itself to its master passion." - Rebecca West

❖ CHAPTER 41 ❖

Grow at Your Own Pace

As I was packing recently, in preparation for a move, I came across an old journal that I kept in 2000 as part of a small mastermind group. It was a bit of a surprise to flip through the pages and read some of the stuff I had written- intentions I had set to work through some things I was struggling with, emotional pain from a betrayal and other desires, longings and experiences I wanted to create.

What surprised me most about reading some of those things is that having since moved so far from that place, it was hard for me to even remember ever being there; it felt foreign, unfamiliar. It was like reading someone else's life. But here I was, twelve years later, and I knew that even though NOW many of those things are no longer relevant for me, back then they were. Very.

Through a lot of inner work, prayer, surrender, and just simply allowing time to apply its healing salve, those issues that were once so big no longer exist.

What a blessing it is, to move through our life, healing, growing, always. Sometimes the growth and healing is so gradual, we don't even feel it happening. I didn't. I'm grateful for today, reading over those expressions of a 29 year-old me, that I took a moment to recognize how far I've come.

I have a memory of finding a butterfly cocoon when I was about ten. It was so exciting and I was very eager to set the butterfly free, I cut the shell open and realized I had killed the creature inside, in my eagerness to rush nature.

We're like that, often, when it comes to our own growth. We are eager to rush nature.

* * * *

❖ TRUTH

Today I invite you to think of the ten-year-younger you. What was she like? What were her longings? How did her heart ache? What were her struggles and pains that once seemed so insurmountable? And where are you now?

❖ DARE

Give yourself credit for the changes and growth you've accomplished– organically, sometimes painfully slow, but real, and true. Sometimes that change, like a blossoming bud, is impossible to notice with the naked eye, but it's happening, whether we can see it or not. For here you are. And it's not where you were. You're better and stronger and wiser. And that's really something worth noticing.

❖ CHAPTER 42 ❖

What's Your Wild Heart Telling You?

Confession time: I am obsessed with a certain performer, and this obsession has fired up my wild heart and feels like lovesickness, even sorta like teen angst, like sheer idolatry. Watching her music videos actually makes my skin hot and tingly and my gives my stomach butterflies.

Florence + The Machine entered my radar two years ago, and instantly fired me up and stirred me in ways I'm still making sense of. I feel shook up, in a really interesting, curious way, and I wanted to peel back that feeling and get to the core of why one particular video was shaking me up to such a yummy, intoxicating, ridiculous degree.

I thought, hey, I'm a coach, why not coach myself? This is how it went.

"Self," I said. "What is it you love about this Florence video?"

"Well, hmm... let me see." I answered. "I love the drama. The lights. The glitter. I love her sexiness. The blatant femininity and sensuality all over this video. The fierceness of her voice, the strength of her stance. The beauty and the grace and strength. The bright, rich colors. I love her costumes, the way she writhes with abandon on a mirrored, lighted, shiny floor... the way she flails around, dancing passionately. I love the fiery soul and unabashed intensity of the song... the angst, the longing, the magical, mystical tones of the harp... shall I go on?"

"No, that's good." And then my coach sat back and smiled. "You are what you love."

I've learned this before. It's been a major component of my coaching practice, helping people discover their life's purpose. It was a telling inquiry tool in my own personal work with Style Statement a few years back.

Quite simply, by closely investigating the very objects and expressions we are drawn to, we are given clues and glimpses into our own authenticity.

These things that stir us up with such intensity are invitations to create MORE of that in our own lives.

After several months of working the Style Statement process with my closest girlfriends, it's no surprise that I discovered my personal two-worded Style Statement to be **"Expressive Fire."**

BINGO. That's why this video SO does it for me. It's a mirror of my own Expressive Fire!

I'm receiving a personalized invitation from the Universe to attend my own Soul's party. To tend to my soul, period. To seek and create and express and BE these very things that I love so dearly about the video:

Emotion

Beauty

Grace

Strength

Glitter, lights, mirrors

Adventure

Drama

Longing

Color

Fierceness

Magic

Mysticism

Passion

Sexiness

Sensuality

Femininity

Fire

Intensity

Okay, Universe, I'm listening.

I graciously ACCEPT the invitation to tend to my soul and find artistic, expressive ways to stoke my own fire.

I am reminded, with deep gratitude, that *the things we love are the things we are.*

It's true. Okay, so maybe I don't have red hair, but I do love to writhe on the floor.

* * * *

❖ TRUTH

And so now I ask you, dear reader, what turns YOU on? What stirs you up? What makes you crazy with intense desire? What ignites you the way this song and video does me?

What do YOU love?

And what does that say about *who you are*?

❖ DARE

I dare you – double dog dare you- to explore the things you are drawn to like a moth to a flame, investigate the things that twist you, peel the layers, and receive the messages about YOU that these things have to offer.

I dare you to accept the invitation to tend to your soul, by first examining what drives you wild. You game?

❖ CHAPTER 43 ❖

Wildly In Love With Life

You get to choose. It's that easy.

People often comment to me that I seem 'happy all the time.' Some of them even seem downright irritated. I know that I am lucky. In spite of family genetics that go back generations that "should" lead me straight into depression, for some strange reason my natural and most comfortable disposition is joy.

I used to worry (okay, I sometimes still do) that my joy might be "too much" for people. That maybe I should tone it down to make people more comfortable. People struggle with real issues and maybe my miss-bright-side ways are salt on the wounds of others. Maybe I should turn my dimmer switch just a little… blah blah blah. and then I decide: fuggit. I have 'real issues' too, just like anyone else. But for the most part, I'm happy, dammit.

I remember the words of Marianne Williamson, *"Your playing small doesn't serve the world. There's nothing enlightened about shrinking so that other people won't feel insecure around you. We are all meant to shine."*

Yesterday on Facebook, I posted the status *"Lisa Carmen is madly in love with her life."* A couple of people cheered me on, a couple others posted responses that seemed to have the underlying sentiment "Yeah, yeah, we know…" And another wanted to know what my secret is; what is there to love so "madly"? And the simplest possible answer I could give was this:

"Figure out what you love to be and what you love to do. Then be and do more of that. I guess that's the short answer."

Yes, I am madly, deeply, wildly in love with Life.

I like to think of Life as my lover. Life and I are having a wild, passionate affair. I am romanced by Life all day long. Right now, as I type this, Life is flirting with me, as wind blows the lusciously green dancing tree branches outside my window, sun beaming through leaves. The music I play while I work is Life singing me a love song, seducing me to dance. When I ate my salad for lunch today, Life was courting me to savor its deliciousness, textures and flavors. And I did. There are opportunities to be madly in love with life everywhere I look, in everything I do. And I'm completely unapologetic about that.

There are opportunities for EACH of us to be madly in love with life, everywhere we look, in everything we do.

When I was a kid and I would complain that I was bored, my dad would say "You're bored because you're boring." While at the time, I thought it seemed a little harsh, his intention has stuck with me my whole life. *I* am responsible for my own happiness.

You are responsible for your own happiness.

And just for the record, I am not happy "all the time." I have my bad days, my bitchy, cranky, for-the-love-of-god-keep- me-away-from-people days. Just like anyone else, I have plenty of pain and less-than-glowing moments. People see what they want to see, and I'm okay with that. After all, the light they see in me is only a reflection of their very own light.

* * * *

❖ TRUTH

So… are you having a love affair with your life? How is life romancing you? And are you being seduced? What do you want more of in your life? What do you want less of? How can you feel wildly in love with life? Remember, it's an inside job. So little of the outside circumstances really make a difference. *What do you want to feel?*

❖ **DARE**

Do something romantic for yourself. Do not wait or expect others to give you the special feelings and experiences you want. Buy yourself flowers. Take yourself out to dinner. Light candles and dance to beautiful music, with the lights out. Experience bliss. Experience what it feels like to be wildly in love with life. Let your life seduce you.

❖ CHAPTER 44 ❖

This Living Fully is Risky Business

this living fully is risky business.

juggling, balancing, wanting it all.

reality:

knowing I have all the time I need

to do the things I want to do

to cultivate the dreams I was born with

to love, to play, to work, to be

what I was meant to be.

knowing the resources

are available and within my reach

for doing what I came here to do.

it's only too late if i I don't start now.

foolishness:

thinking I have all the time in the world

to do the things I want to do

to cultivate the dreams I was born with.

excepting inspiration to fall from the sky

onto my lap.

investing half way in my own divine purpose

to love, play, work,

to do what I came here to do.

postponing my efforts

conserving my energies

wasting my time

on fruitless activities,

empty relationships,

safe distractions

waiting for the "perfect moment to start."

acting as if I own "forever"

as if my days are unnumbered.

as if tomorrow is promised.

I am ready to risk. I am ready to leap.

I am ready to unfold this story, unfold my wings and take flight.

* * * *

❖ TRUTH

What are you waiting for? What experience have you put on hold for the right time, another time? How have you been holding back in life? Journal or share your answers with the Facebook group.

❖ DARE

It's time to take a leap. Stop playing safe. Take a risk. Do what you have been waiting to do. No more excuses. The time is now.

❖ CHAPTER 45 ❖

I am the Boss of Me

I am ridiculously happy.

I used to feel a certain sort of shyness or hesitancy when it came to sharing my ridiculously happy happiness... that I had to tone it down, dim it, whisper instead of shout, just in case someone was miserable, it wouldn't be very kind of me to be so...um... so happy.

But you know what? I don't feel that way anymore. Because my happiness robs no one of theirs. And neither does yours.

You are entitled to every bit of juicy joy and more than you can possibly squeeze out of life.

And if you're NOT experiencing joy, pleasure and deep-down in-your-soul, in-your-bones, in-your-gut happiness... I heard the simplest quote today on a radio program, a truth so obvious, yet powerful:

"If you aren't happy with who you are and what you do, change it."

"After all," adds my boyfriend, Matt, "You aren't a tree."

Yes, it's true. I am the boss of me. You are the boss of you. You and only you are the solution, are the antidote, the cure, the magician, the sorceress, the lord, the queen of your kingdom. If you need more happy... make it. If you want more excitement, do more exciting things. If you're lonely, go meet more people. If you hate your job, get a new one or find ways to love the one you have.

Notice the verbs: Go. Do. Get. Find. Love.

That means action. And action means you have to act.

Wanting, waiting, desiring, longing, whining, complaining... they all have their place, as does misery, as the seed of change, the beginning of reinvention. Misery is after all one of the most motivating forces in the world...

I implore you: If you aren't loving your life, do what you need to do to love your life. Because Life wants to love YOU.

* * * *

❖ TRUTH

Rate the areas of your life listed below on a scale of 1 to 10, 1 being "pretty miserable", 10 being "ridiculously satisfied." Then answer each question.

Career

Is my job rewarding?
Does it reflect my values?
Do I have opportunity for advancement?

Money

Do I earn enough and live within my means?
Do I save enough?
Am I planning for financial freedom?

Health

Am I generally fit and well?
Do I eat healthily?
Do I exercise regularly?

Significant other/Romance

Do I have/want a soul mate?
Do we share values and intimacy?
Am I nurturing the relationship we have with each other?

Friends and Family

Do I have/want a close circle of friends?
Do I spend enough time with family and friends?
Do I value the relationship we have with each other?

Fun and Recreation

Do I have fun often?
Do I know how to relax?
Do I enjoy sports or have hobbies?

Personal Growth

Am I continually learning new things?
Do I enjoy new opportunities for growth?
Are the things I do growing me as a person?

Physical Environment

Do I like the area in which I live?
Is my home comfortable, tidy and warm?
Do I keep my appearance smart?
Is my car serviced and reliable?

From www.pure-coaching.com

❖ DARE

Look closely at your answers and evaluate your life from an "outsiders" view, as if you were a coach. Which areas stand out as the most needing of attention? Select the most pressing one or two areas and create a list of things that need to change. What can you change right now? What small action can you take? What can you stop doing, effective immediately. You call the shots. You are in charge. No one is responsible for your happiness except you. And you deserve to be ridiculously happy.

♣ CHAPTER 46 ♣

What if Pleasure IS the Path?

"*What pleases you?*" was the question. And when Joanie drew the slip of paper from the basket during our sacred circle, she read it, and paused. Then she began to cry. We sat and held space for her as she let the feelings move through her, and then she spoke her answer:

"*I have no idea.*"

In one way or another, each of the women at the retreat could relate. *You probably can, too.* At some point in all of our lives, we wander away from the core of who we are and what we love. What we enjoy. What feels good.

In all of our busyness and to-dos and tweeting and texting and replying and surviving and doing for others (*we're SO good at that!*) we can lose access to our essence, to the pleasures and indulgences and sensory thrills that we used to enjoy… to the goose bumps and surges of joy and titillations of life, love, connection, nature, art, beauty, sex, sensuality… all the things in our world that make us feel alive.

And then, when we've wandered so far from who we are, it feels more like **who we WERE**, lost our connection to our very essence, so far away that what we desire or enjoy or need feels more like memory than fact, we can get triggered by something as simple as a song playing on the radio that takes us back, or a question in circle at a retreat or a delicious piece of dark chocolate with chili and lime that reminds us that there is something more… way more… to life than what we are experiencing.

Pleasure is more than just a novelty, **it's your birthright.**

You showed up in that body, with those senses and those feelings, and the ability to pop goose bumps from your skin and get melty gooey lovey dovey if you're in the right mood, and smell all kinds of things, some scents more pleasurable than others.

Your senses are divine.

Not just divine. ***Your ability to experience pleasure IS Divinity!*** It's not just a scenic route on the path to spirituality or enlightenment. In fact, I believe that **pleasure IS the path**. *Ah... what do you think about that?*

I don't care what you learned as a little girl about denying yourself of pleasure. It was a lie. It doesn't matter what they taught you in Sunday school about "fleshly" pleasure being separate from holiness. It's B.S. **Flesh IS holy**. Holy, holy, life is yummy!

* * *

❖ TRUTH

What about a doctrine of desire? What if feeling good was your religion? What if experiencing pleasure, lots and lots of it, was your holiest prayer of gratitude? Hmmm...

Go ahead, think about what pleases you.

What feels good? What do you like to touch? Taste? Smell? What is beautiful to you? What are your yummiest experiences? What lights your fire? Make a list.

And then, today, pick one thing and...

❖ DARE

Experience it. Feel it. Taste it. Smell it. Do it.

❖ CHAPTER 47 ❖

Shut Up and Let Me Be Happy

We all have them. The "Inner Mean Girls" (or boys) that live inside our head and compete for attention with compelling reasons as to why we should not be happy, how incapable we are of being great, how imperfect our bodies are, what terrible daughters/mothers/wives/friends/sisters we are, why we are not enough and how undeserving we are of most good things. WHEW.

I can't say I've gotten complete and total control of these voices, but I am making dramatic shifts. The first step: by simply recognizing them, I begin to dissolve their power.

What's super cool is that the more familiar I am with them, their boring old arguments, their lame attempts at raining on my parade, their true scaredy-cat natures, I am getting better at spotting them a mile away, and I'm getting really good at stopping them in their tracks.

This is how I know:

The other day, on a particularly grateful, serene quiet morning, I sat in my favorite chair, with my coffee and my journal, basking in the happiness of that moment and my life.

I wrote *"I love my life. To be alive, to be living this life is such a gift. I'm so grateful for all the blessings..."* and then, suddenly, there she was, the "Inner Mean Girl" I'll call Bubbles, cuz she's really good at bursting them. She said to me, while I was writing...

"Oh yeah? Well, what about..." and prepared to lay into me with all the creative, colorful and compelling reasons I should not be happy.

And this is how I know I have made dramatic progress:

In my mind, I quickly cut her off and without even thinking, said **"SHUT UP AND LET ME BE HAPPY."**

I didn't even let her finish her sentence! I don't even know what she was going to say! I just wasn't in the mood to hear it, and dammit, I'm entitled to happiness without her stupid "Yeah-Buts."

Maybe you have your own "Bubbles..."

Even though our mamas taught us that nice girls don't interrupt, I say screw it. I say cut her off. Shut her up. Interrupt her. After all, you've let her have her way with you for long enough, haven't you?

Stake your claim to happiness, stand your ground and tell your "Inner Mean Girl" to shut the hell up next time she starts her crap. I'm not saying she'll run off and never come back. But this is the way to begin... the rewiring of the brain, the new thought patterns and that conscious, CHOSEN HAPPINESS that is your divine birthright.

We DO get to choose our thoughts, you know. One interruption at a time.

* * * *

❖ TRUTH

When you hear your "Inner Mean Girl," what are some of the things she says to you? Write them down. Your Inner Mean Girl has a personality. Give her a name. Rude Rhoda? Scaredy Cat Sophie? Grudge Grrl? Bully Beeyatch?

Become aware of her when she speaks to you. *"Oh there she goes again, Bully Beeyatch. Telling me what I can and can't do. Sigh..."*

Becoming aware of her is the first step!

❖ DARE

Begin to question her motives. Her back story. Fight back. Initiate a coup. Resist. Thank you for her concern. Reassign her to a better role. For example, Worry Wart Wanda may be good for analyzing your decisions and giving her vote. She does not get to run the company. Take away her power. Give her the pink slip. Flip her the finger.

❖ CHAPTER 48 ❖

Watch Out Below, Plummeting Moods!

I've been noticing something interesting lately. I've been starting out my days on a high vibration, fiercely grateful, mindfully approaching every task with presence, joy… All ooey gooey and overflowing with love. And I move through my day, completing tasks. Or not. Bouncing around from one priority to another. One diversion to another.

And then, at some point, BAM. I crash. I don't just crash. I plummet. My mood shifts *dramatically*. I go from joyous bearer of light to bitch on wheels. Just like that. Or so it seems.

I look at my sweet Facebook posts from the morning and roll my eyes at myself. I think bad thoughts. I make careless mistakes. I'm stressed and tired and off-kilter.

All that overflowing, ooey gooey love has coagulated and turned into something much less appetizing, viscous and dry. I am hard and closed and cranky. I dislike. I complain. I worry. I feel overwhelmed and feral. Not fit for human interaction.

What is this shift? Why does it happen? So suddenly it seems, yet maybe if I look closely, not so sudden at all.

For a while I thought it was a sugar crash. Or a hormonal imbalance. Or demon possession. But today, I'm realizing it's something way more subtle and insidious. And really, quite simple…

I haven't checked in with myself.

All tangled up in the doing, going, creating, replying, forwarding, posting, planning, I've wandered away from myself.

It makes perfect sense. I start my day with ritual. I make my coffee. I light candles. I journal. I read. I pray. It's no wonder i'm full of love and light!

And then, little by little, I disconnect from myself, from source. I forget to check in. I ignore the desire to stretch. I hold my pee for ridiculous lengths of time.

I've decided here and now to return to a daily practice. A simple practice called stopping. Remember lunch hours? I used to have them in corporate America. I kinda miss those.

I will check in. Ask myself what I want, feel and need. I will tune in, jump off the grid for a few minutes. Refuel. Start my midday the way I start my morning. Wow. What a concept. And why not? I heard a woman say to another woman who was complaining about her back-breaking busy schedule… "Wow… Who on earth is responsible for treating you that way? Who's the tyrant that manages your schedule?" Yes, it was sarcastic. In a loving sort of way.

"You get out of balance because you aren't listening to your inner life, because you aren't meeting your challenges of your life with any input from the inside. You haven't given yourself enough time to know what you think or feel."
- Jennifer Louden, "Comfort Secrets for Busy Women"

I'm ready to try something new. To restore my balance midday in order to experience more joy.

What shifts or changes are you ready to make?

I'm off to retore and renew now… See you on the other side of my day. Most likely, in a much better mood.

* * *

❖ TRUTH

What time of the month, week or day do you usually feel yourself fizzling, getting cranky or losing your steam?

❖ DARE

The next time you feel your energy or spirit waning, stop what you are doing, remove yourself physically from the situation and do something kind and gentle for yourself. Reboot. Refuel. Recharge. I dare you.

❖ CHAPTER 49 ❖

You're Sexy and You Know It

*"When I walk in the spot (yeah), this is what I see (ok)
Everybody stops and they staring at me
I got passion in my pants and I ain't afraid to show it...
I'm sexy and I know it."*
    -LMFAO

You've heard the song. Maybe you've even sung along in your car, or danced with friends to it. It's goofy and it's catchy and my goodness, is it loaded with bravado (*"No shoes, no shirt, and I STILL get serviced"*, for example...) But there's something in the over-the-top arrogance that the soul recognizes. *Yeah.* **I said soul.**

Have you ever felt so sure of yourself, so attractive and on top of your game, confident and put together to the point where your body and your soul are in complete alignment, when your senses are providing a direct line to your spirit and you're abuzz with reality? *When you are sexy, and you know it?*

You may have experienced it dancing, making love, climaxing alone, celebrating with friends, completing a project that turned out better than you even expected. Showing up fully for loved ones who need you. Flirting with your new crush, or your husband of 25 years. You know the feeling.

It's when who you are on the inside reflects who you are on the outside. It's when your senses are fully engaged. it's when your experience of yourself becomes High Definition, and the world and everything in it shines brighter for that reason. It's when connection, real connection- heart to heart, soul to soul connection happens, it's where curiosity meets longing and you've never felt more alive.

You're sexy and you know it.

If you're not experiencing this at all, or you can't remember the last time... it may be time for a shift.

Life was meant to be savored. Life is longing to seduce you. There is so much passion, so much richness and flavor and color and texture all around, and guess what? It's for you. When you are engaged, fully engaged, with life and the world and yourself, you can't help to experience a little bravado. Mixed with a tender humility, you feel WOW. You ARE wow, embodied.

Life is a passionate lover, and it matters not if you have a human lover or if you simply decide to let Life itself be your mate, with all of its surprises, seduction, romance, adventures and gifts.

Feeling sexy is your birthright. And Life has a crush on you. Go on. *Flirt.*

* * *

❖ TRUTH

What makes you feel sexy? What makes you come alive? When's the last time you were titillated? Write in your journal or share with the Facebook group.

❖ DARE

Do something sexy! Today. Report back to "base camp" with your tale.

❖ CHAPTER 50 ❖

What if I Told You?

What if I told you that you are not your mistakes?

What if I told you that there are no mistakes?

What if I told you that every so-called detour, distraction, poor choice or bad decision you've ever made was actually exactly right because it brought you to exactly here, exactly you, exactly in this moment, and exactly NOW is perfect.

What if I told you there is nothing wrong with you?

What if I told you that any wisdom you seek in gurus and therapists and churches and teachers and philosophers and coaches is already within you.

That the gurus and therapists and teachers and churches and philosophers and coaches, the good ones at least, will never take credit for "fixing you" or "saving you" or "delivering you". They are simply showing you a mirror of your own brilliance and reminding you of what your soul already knows, has always known and will always know (but sometimes we all need reminding.)

What if I told you that you have, within you, every single strength, tool, trait and ability to handle everything and anything that you should face or have faced, in your life?

What if I told you that there is no such thing as "soul healing" because it is impossible to damage a soul because your soul is divine and divinity is indestructible, unrelenting, perfectly perfect perfection?

What if I told you that any wounds or so-called "damage" that you think you carry from what was done or not done, what was given or not given, what was said or not said to you when you were a tiny child or an angsty teen or a hungry seeker did not nor could not touch your soul and within you is the perfection of your divine essence, always, no matter what, forever and ever amen?

What if I told you that you are brilliant, and beautiful and amazing and perfect, just as you are? That you are a bright and radiant star and that you were born to shine?

What if I told you that you, my sweet, beautiful friend, are exactly right. Right now. As is. You are the I am. You are divinity incarnate.

Would you believe me?

* * * *

❖ TRUTH

Which of the statements above felt the most difficult to embrace? Does it feel opposite of a belief you hold? Is that belief working for you? What would it take for you to ditch the old belief, and experiment with a brand new one?

❖ DARE

Pick one that you would like to claim. Claim it. Write it on sticky-notes and stick them on your bathroom mirror, your monitor, in your car. For example...

There is nothing wrong with me.
I am not my mistakes.
My soul is perfectly perfect.

❖ CHAPTER 51 ❖

I Will Not Abandon Myself

I know how to be here

in this gray place,

so familiar in its charm-less charm

I've learned how to be here

in this dark space

and not be afraid,

I know how to be here, now.

I know when it shows up

uninvited visitor.

the best thing to do

is to take its coat,

offer it a seat,

a snack, a footrest.

I will not resist its embrace

I will not run from its force

I've been down that road before.

I will not abandon myself.

instead I will stay.

I will be.

I will know

that everything changes

and that the light

is defined by the dark.

This is the poem I scribble in my journal on a dark day. Weighed down by the heaviness of what I easily recognize now as depression, all I want to do is sleep. When I'm not sleeping, I'm fantasizing about sleeping. I cancel meetings and lunches with girlfriends because I don't want to talk to anyone or get dressed or brush my teeth. I want to crawl under a rock or a blanket and sleep 'til springtime. Maybe it's the change in seasons, maybe it's hormonal, maybe it's chemical, maybe it's Mercury in retrograde, maybe it's this, maybe it's that, maybe it doesn't even matter. Melancholic and mopey, I have no 'reasonable' explanation for these feelings, they're just here, hanging over me, blocking my view of the light. I cannot feel the light. I want to run. I want to hide.

But this time, I don't. Because things are different now. I'm trying something different these days. I am a scientist in my soul's laboratory. I am experimenting with a new idea. *This time, I will stay with these feelings.*

I have spent so much of my life running from my negative emotions, hiding, numbing from anything that felt bad, completely convinced that feeling bad was BAD, and that bad feelings were to be avoided. I had a hundred ways to avoid a bad feeling. Anything to leave that bad feeling. On some days, I'd try all hundred.

"Cheer up!" a well-meaning friend tells me, while I waffle in this mud puddle of murky emotions, splashing around, getting some of my muck in his eyes. Yes, he means well, yet I know (finally) that 'cheering up' is not what I need- that's how I got myself into the habitual behaviors and shadow comforts that I have spent years weaning myself from in the first place.

Instead, I have vowed to not abandon myself. To not turn my back on this dark feeling in me. To just sit with my emotion, that is my challenge, to just be with this ache, this hollow feeling, that is my sole job some days, and it's takes more energy than I care to admit, some days. It's so much easier (and familiar!) to hide, to run, to numb, to bail. Instead, this time, I acknowledge the yuckiness. This time, I don't turn away from it, but simply hold it like a colicky baby. I rock it back and forth and whisper soothing words. *There, there. You're okay, baby. I'm here...*

Richard Moss in his work "The Mandala of Being" talks about the difference between being *in* your feelings, and your feelings being in *you*. We so often buy into the illusion that our feelings can actually engulf us, swallow us, that we can lose ourselves in them. Moss gently urges readers instead *to be a safe place for their feelings*, to create spaciousness around the feeling, no matter how dark and ugly the feeling might be, and I am now driven by the challenge of discovering what a life lived this way will look like. I am experimenting, all right. *I will not abandon myself.*

What I also know is this: When I create a safe space for my feelings, it turns out these feelings are not as terrible or ugly or awful or deadly as I imagined them. They're more hungry-baby than scary-monster. Most of the time, all they want is to be acknowledged, to be felt, to be held. They will not destroy me, or engulf me, because *they are just feelings*, they are mine, I hold them inside of me, and lo and behold, I am finally a safe place for my feelings.

I heard a woman on the radio talking about her inner work, the way that she had learned to accept all of her feelings with love and compassion, after a lifetime of rejecting her 'bad' emotions. Mmm... I could relate. Just a little. At the end of the show, she was asked to share her motto, and I loved her answer so much I've now adopted it as my own.

If I would have heard this woman ten years ago, five years ago, last year even, I probably wouldn't have gotten it- it would have been just beyond my understanding, like hearing a foreign language, as I was still so passionately dedicated to avoiding and rejecting my own 'bad' feelings. (But because we receive exactly what we need, what we are ready
for, exactly *when* we are ready for it, I *didn't* hear it ten or five years ago, I heard it the other day.)

She said: *"All feelings are welcome here."* And I thought, for the first time in my life, yes. Yes, they are.

* * * *

❖ TRUTH

Are you a safe place for any feeling? Can you create spaciousness around a darker emotion, so that it is cushioned and softened?

What emotions do you find the most difficult to be with? What can you do to stay with yourself, the next time this feeling arises?

❖ DARE

Create an alternate plan, a strategy for being a safe place for yourself when your next funk comes along. For example...

- Instead of reaching for the chips and dip, I will reach for my journal.

- Instead of reaching for wine, I will reach for incense, candles and quiet.

- Instead of lashing out at the kids, I will step outside and breathe deeply, until I am re-centered.

Then, the next time you are feeling funky, experiment with your new strategies, knowing and trusting that you are indeed, a safe place for every feeling.

❖ CHAPTER 52 ❖

Buckle Your Seat Belt. Hold Onto Your Hat. It's Time.

Whoa.

As my 17-year old daughter would say, DUDE.

Do you feel what I feel?

A quickening, an intensity, the electricity, the energy, the pulsing urgency of a new world, birthing forth, bursting forward, the reality that nothing is the same, that everything has changed, that it's time, it's time, it's time... and we, dear sisters, are at the center of it. We are tapping in, we are busting out, we are done playing small. We are the mothers, we are the midwifes, the godmothers, the goddesses, here to rock, here to manifest a brand new planet. Here to save the world. YES. I am a superhero. And so are you.

Virtually every woman I know is experiencing some sort of shift in her life. Do any of these sound like you?

- Leaping from trapeze to trapeze, without a safety net?
- Shedding old skins that no longer serve or fit? Maybe your relationship is completing itself, you no longer connect with old friends the way you once did, you're itchy in outdated roles, jobs and commitments that are ready to be released...
- Doing crazy, bold, adventurous things you never could have imagined, and inspiring others in the process?

- Soul stretching so intensely that if your soul was a belly, it'd have stretch marks?
- Feeling the strange urge to completely upheave your life?
- Attracting new people, circumstances and opportunities that are "SOOOOO YOU" by complete so-called "chance"?
- Practically flipped inside-out with longing, desire, stirrings that are unexplainable and palpable?
- You feel like "It's TIME" but you're not exactly sure what it's time for?

Well sister, it *is* time. It's time for each and everyone of us to step up. To stop pretending we're ordinary when we are anything but. To stop dimming our light so that others feel 'comfortable' around us. To stop hiding our brilliance, to ditch our excuses, to walk through our fears, to challenge others, to claim our divine place in this divine time, because it IS time.

If we were superheroes, our emergency light signal would be beaming from headquarters, shining in the dark night sky. Actually, guess what? We are superheroes, and the super signal IS shining in the dark night sky.

It's time to save the world. No pressure.

Don't worry- you already have every gift, every resource, every ability you need to do your part- it's already in you. It's why you came here, after all. You already got the hook up.

You heal the world by healing your self. You inspire others by inspiring yourself. You light the world ablaze when your heart and your purpose and your activities, choices and relations are aligned with your heart and your purpose.

Your days of playing small are over. It's time to shine your fullest, brightest, boldest radiance. Unleash your greatness. Unfurl your magic.

Are you with me? Let's do this.

"We will never again be the former version of ourselves. All that we have left is to become our future selves."
- Lisa Steadman

* * * *

❖ TRUTH

Which of the bulleted statements above feel most like you and your current life?

What is being called forth from you?

How are you shifting into a higher version of yourself?

What is the next step?

❖ DARE

Take that step.

Quit that job.

Have that conversation.

Write that letter.

Form that alliance.

Start that coup.

Heal that wound.

Release that habit.

Are you ready?

Step into your brilliance.

It's time. Do it.

I dare ya.

ACKNOWLEDGMENTS

Deep and immeasurable gratitude to the friends and loved ones who held the vision of this book with me, supported and encouraged me and dared me to step into this new space, of being an author, a dream I have held since the age of four, a dream made manifest now. You know who you are. I am forever grateful.

Special thanks to the countless authors, poets and teachers who have inspired along the way, many who I have quoted in this book, including Debbie Ford, Mark Nepo, Mary Oliver, Tori Amos, Florence + the Machine, Danielle LaPorte, Lisa Steadman, Richard Moss, Christine Arylo, Amy Ahlers, Marianne Williamson, Erica Jong, Anais Nin, Gregg Levoy, Oriah, Geneen Roth, and Abraham-Hicks.

ABOUT THE AUTHOR

Lisa Carmen is a zealous, fire-starting, purpose, passion and pleasure junkie. She's the creator/curator of SacredSexyU, and is a coach, writer, workshop facilitator, event producer and performer. In 2009, her life took a crazy turn once she performed her first burlesque strip-tease for 500 people... "I realized just how brave and powerful I was, and that I was capable of anything." She now facilitates that life-changing adventure for other women, in her popular course "The Burlesque Experience." She lives in Dallas, Texas and enjoys a beautiful, colorful life with her daughter and fiance.

You can learn more at www.sacredsexyu.com.

"The body's a mirror of heaven:
Its energies make angels jealous.
Our purity astounds seraphim.
Devils shiver at our nerve."
– Rumi

Made in the USA
Charleston, SC
10 January 2016